Will Brexit Damage our Security and Defence?

Simon Duke

Will Brexit Damage our Security and Defence?

The Impact on the UK and EU

palgrave
macmillan

Simon Duke
Maastricht University
Maastricht, The Netherlands

ISBN 978-3-319-96106-4   ISBN 978-3-319-96107-1   (eBook)
https://doi.org/10.1007/978-3-319-96107-1

Library of Congress Control Number: 2018950269

Cover illustration: Stefan_Alfonso / Getty Images

Printed on acid-free paper

This Palgrave Macmillan imprint is published by the registered company Springer Nature
Switzerland AG
The registered company address is: Gewerbestrasse 11, 6330 Cham, Switzerland

To the memory of my father
William Whamond Duke 1925–2017

The original version of this book was revised: Figure 1.1 and Figure 2.1 have been updated. The correction to this book is available at https://doi.org/10.1007/978-3-319-96107-1_6

PREFACE

Writing anything about the UK's departure from the EU (Brexit) could be deemed foolhardy, especially when the nature of the UK's relations with the EU are subject to ongoing negotiation. This brief volume does not try and predict what will happen, but it does ask what the likely impact of Brexit might be upon the UK and EU's security and defence and the options faced by both parties. This book has also been written in the hope that it will contribute to the ongoing debates surrounding Brexit in an informed and analytical manner. It is also intended to be a modest contribution to a hitherto under researched aspect of European integration; that of disintegration and its consequences. While the issue at hand is Brexit, the complexities and consequences of disengagement and withdrawal will hopefully provide wider salutary lessons for the EU itself, NATO and transatlantic relations.

With the political sensitivity surrounding Brexit in mind, every effort has been made to accurately reflect official positions as well as to offer balanced representation of the public, think tank and academic debates surrounding the topic at hand. The book has also been deliberately written to try and reflect the possible implications for both the UK *and* the EU— Brexit is not only about the UK and any agreement on security and defence will depend upon mutual interests.

Such an endeavour inevitably has its challenges, especially since much of the academic output has yet to catch up with the ongoing debates surrounding Brexit due to the inevitable lag in publication involved with books and journals. The new Palgrave Macmillan 'Essentials' series therefore offers the ideal vehicle for something that is brief, topical and that can hopefully be of use in the wider public debates as the UK heads towards departure from the EU in March 2019. While it could be argued that in-depth analysis will have to wait until the nature of the 'deal' becomes apparent, this volume is offered in the belief that there is still the need to think through the security and defence implications of Brexit *now*, rather than later. This also implies that the argumentation in the book is empiri-cal in nature, directed primarily towards policy-makers and others inter-ested in shaping decisions—although it is hoped that it will also be of more than passing interest to academic colleagues.

This book is not written in the belief that security and defence issues will be a deal-breaker for the UK or the EU. Inevitably, trade, migration and borders will be priorities (although they too have their security implications). But, for the EU, Brexit comes at a sensitive moment when issues of security and defence are not only near or at the top of its agenda, but are central to efforts to relaunch wider public enthusiasm for the European project. This may well give the UK some leverage in its negotiations, but whether it is worthy of a 'deep and special partnership with the EU that goes beyond existing third country arrangements', especially when the UK has been dis-tinctly unenthusiastic about the development of security and defence at the European level over the last decade or so, is a key issue. The UK's ambition is to negotiate a security treaty with the EU, based primarily upon an appeal to common values and challenges. While the shape of any eventual treaty is not clear, this book aims to highlight some of the challenges that will face both parties along the path to what will hopefully be new arrangements that will shape the EU and UK's security relations for decades to come.

I would like to briefly thank Jemima Warren at Palgrave Macmillan for giving me the chance to be one of the pioneers of this new series and for putting her faith me. My thanks are also due for the patience of my family, especially my wife Roberta, for tolerating the obsessiveness that inevitably accompanies writing on such a topic. I would also like to thank a number of academic colleagues with whom I have had the chance to exchange views or, more generally, benefit from their own writing on the topic (without implying that they necessarily agree with all that follows). Thomas Christiansen deserves particular mention in this regard. I hope that you will recognise your suggestions and, in spite of all of the assis-tance that I have received, any errors remain entirely my own.

Honthem, Netherlands   Simon Duke
July, 2018

CONTENTS

LIST OF FIGURES

CHAPTER 1

The Role of Security and Defence Before and After the June 2016 Referendum

The campaign leading up to the June 2016 referendum was primarily fought over immigration, sovereignty, the economy and a more general dissatisfaction with politics. Divisions over security played in the background with the Leave campaign arguing that full control of immigration and our borders was vital, while the Remain campaign stressed the importance of collaboration and data-sharing with our EU partners to address trans-national threats. Interestingly, as Home Secretary, Theresa May also saw the potential link between immigration and security and came down on the 'Remain' side of the debate. Both pro-Leave and pro-Remain campaigns were able to evoke recent terrorist attacks in their respective political agendas but to opposite ends.

Successive UK governments, including that of Prime Minister David Cameron, have consistently been at the forefront of attempts to ensure that the EU, especially on questions of security and defence, should not be subject to more influence or control by the Commission or the European Parliament (so-called 'communitarisation'). There were instances where the UK played an obstructive role, such as the blocking of a functional operations headquarters at the EU level or, for seven years, any increase of the European Defence Agency (EDA) budget. Historically, the UK has often been an 'awkward partner', to quote the title of a leading book on the UK's role in the EU (George 1997). Cameron's demands for a special status for the UK had deep historical resonance, but this came on top of the UK's 'opt-outs' on the Schengen

© The Author(s) 2019
S. Duke, *Will Brexit Damage our Security and Defence?*,
https://doi.org/10.1007/978-3-319-96107-1_1

Agreement, Economic and Monetary Union (EMU), the EU Charter of Fundamental Rights and the area of freedom, security and justice—opt-outs that were not available to the newer EU members who joined after 2004. Cameron's demands were eventually agreed to by the other EU leaders on the understanding that, on this basis, he would campaign 'heart and soul to keep Britain inside a reformed European Union' following his January 2013 pledge to give the people a simple choice of remaining in the EU under the new terms, or to leave (Cameron 2015).

In a major pre-vote speech Cameron insisted that, 'Britain has a fundamental national interest in maintaining common purpose in Europe to avoid future conflict between European countries. And that requires British leadership, and for Britain to remain a member' (Cameron 2016). Patriotic references to Blenheim, Trafalgar and Waterloo and two World Wars were used to highlight Britain's 'heroism'. Kenneth Clarke, a well-known pro-Europe Conservative, wrote that 'Britain's political voice depends on our role as a leading and influential member of the EU' and he observed that when the EU governments agree on political and economic policies, 'they will remain a superpower to influence the Americans, the Russians, Indians and Chinese over the coming decades' (Clarke 2015). Those campaigning for Remain subsequently echoed the connection between security and prosperity made by Clarke and Cameron (Whitman 2016a, 1).

The pro-EU campaign, *Britain Stronger in Europe*, was formally launched on 12 October 2015 and from the outset argued that, 'Being in the EU gives Britain a more powerful role in the world and a say in major global decisions affecting you and your family' (Britain Stronger in Europe 2015). The campaign included former Chief of the General Staff Sir Peter Wall, as well as former Prime Ministers John Major, Gordon Brown and Tony Blair. The campaign made extensive use of prominent experts, including on security where the common message was that Britain's security is enhanced by EU membership and would therefore be damaged in various ways by an exit. But, the establishment was clearly split.

The *Vote Leave* campaign, also founded in October 2015, was less specific about Britain's global role but argued that border control and migration were key issues for Britain's security and that, on defence, cooperation is good but centralisation of control over defence in Brussels is not (Vote

Leave 2015).[1] The Brexit campaign, most notably Boris Johnson, was able to largely side-line discussion of the UK's post-Brexit security role by pointing out that an EU foreign and defence policy would only serve to undermine NATO and UK ties with the US. Falklands war veteran Major General Julian Thompson and General Sir Michael Rose, a former SAS head, also came out in favour of Brexit, with Thompson arguing against being 'dominated by people who we do not elect', while the latter argued that 'European law has already seriously undermined UK's combat effectiveness' (Associated Press 2016). Rose joined Johnson and others in arguing that European defence can 'manifestly be better made solely through NATO than by trying to spread our limited resources too thinly, in order to include European defence and security policy initiatives into the UK's defence programme' (Associated Press 2016).

Turning to internal security Sir Richard Dearlove, a former MI6 head, claimed that Britain's open borders policy was against the UK's interests and that post-Brexit bilateral ties could easily prevail over any losses suffered from withdrawing from the European Police Agency (Europol) (Robertson 2016). More generally, Dearlove (2016) argued that Britain gives much more when it comes to intelligence and security matters and that 'its intelligence and security community is, and will certainly remain, the strongest and most mature in Europe'. This helped underpin the later assumption that the UK not only has the right to a deep and special relationship with the EU post-Brexit, but that this should be one that is not available to any other third country.

The Leave lobby also frequently invoked alleged plans to create a 'European army' as proof of the EU's federalist tendencies. Although many analysts have dismissed this as a mythical fabrication of the less than scrupulous British press, it is worth noting that the President of the European Commission, Jean-Claude Juncker, called for the creation of a European army in March 2015 as a way of conveying to Russia 'that we are serious about defending the values of the European Union' (Deutsche Welle 2015). The UK's former Defence Secretary, Michael Fallon, opposed any attempts to create an EU army since it risked undermining NATO which 'must remain the cornerstone of our defence and the defence of Europe'

---

[1] Vote Leave and Britain Stronger in Europe were not designated by the Electoral Commission as the official campaign groups until 13 April 2016. Numerous other groups party-based groups, interest groups and professional groups campaigned in support of the official remain and leave campaigns.

(Fallon 2016). The toxic invocation of the 'European army' became a lode star of the Eurosceptical security and defence debate and one that proved remarkably difficult to debunk, due in part to the distrust of 'experts' promoted by Michael Gove, the UK's Justice Secretary. As a prominent Brexit campaigner Gove opined that 'people in this country have had enough of experts' (Mance 2016). Although he was referring specifically to the post-referendum economic plans being promoted by the Brexit campaign, his comment only served to lower the standards of informed debate.

The Balance of Competences

The respective sides in the Brexit campaign adopted positions that largely ignored the outcome of a major UK government review of the balance of competences between the EU and the UK. The review took place over three semesters, starting in April 2012 and concluding in autumn 2014. On 'foreign policy' (which included the security and defence aspects) the review concluded that 'the balance of competences lies squarely with the Member States' (UK Government 2013, 5). The evidence gathered in this domain led to the conclusion that 'it was strongly in the UK's interests to work through the EU in a number of policy areas' (UK Government 2013, 6). The key benefits were identified as:

> ...increased impact from acting in concert with 27 other countries; greater influence with non-EU powers, derived from our position as a leading EU country; the international weight of the EU's single market, including its power to deliver commercially beneficial trade agreements; the reach and magnitude of EU financial instruments, such as for development and economic partnerships; the range and versatility of the EU's tools, as compared with other international organisations; and the EU's perceived political neutrality, which enables it to act in some cases where other countries or international organisations might not.

The review also noted that there were also comparative disadvantages, such as:

> ...challenges in formulating strong, clear strategy; uneven leadership; institutional divisions, and a complexity of funding instruments, which can impede implementation of policy; and sometimes slow or ineffective decision-making, due to complicated internal relationships and differing interests. (UK Government 2013, 6)

In a similar vein, a Report by the House of Commons Foreign Affairs Committee expressed the concern that leaving the EU might suggest a 'retreat' from world affairs or a 'shrinking' of the UK's international role (House of Commons 2016, 17). It was also noted that the UK's potential departure could worsen the EU's ongoing existential crises which, in turn, could have knock-on effects for the UK. Several ironies were also noted, such as Brexit necessitating the expansion of the UK's diplomatic representation in Brussels (with 50 new diplomatic posts in Europe being created by reassignments), contrary to the widespread assumption that the UK's post-Brexit presence in Brussels would be down-sized (Mance 2018). At the very least, the prospect of a UK withdrawal was seen as a precursor to a 'wide-ranging review of the UK's position in the world' (House of Commons 2016, 21). A number of those contributing to the report, such as Charles Grant, argued that even prior to the announcement of the referendum, 'Britain has become more inward-looking and been less willing to engage and lead the EU and shape EU foreign policies' (House of Commons 2016, 22).

Given the background role played by security concerns in the pre-referendum debates, the assumption was that 'withdrawal from the EU should arguably have a relatively minor impact on the UK's long-term defensive posture and capabilities' (House of Commons 2016, 26). This was in part due to the intergovernmental nature of the EU's Common Security and Defence Policy (CSDP) alongside the perception that it 'has never been central to the UK's defence effort' (House of Lords 2018). The prospect of the UK cooperating closely with the EU on security and defence was seen as realistic, given the prominent role played by the national capitals. The impact of Brexit was also downplayed due to the fact that the UK's role in NATO will continue to be of importance and, in the event of Brexit, it may even lead to enhanced cooperation with NATO allies who are also EU members. Brexit would also allow for the continuation of bilateral cooperation, such as that with France on the basis of the 2010 Lancaster House Treaties.

The bombings at Zaventem airport and Maalbeek metro in Brussels on 22 March 2016, in which over thirty civilians died, not only moved security closer to the centre of the pre-referendum debates but also led to the increasing polarisation of the leave and remain campaigns. On the eve of the referendum vote on 23 June 2016 the polls suggested a narrow majority for remain (at 48%) over leave (46%) (Financial Times 2016). But with the normal margin of error (±3%) and 6% undecided, all bets were off. A pamphlet distributed to each UK household by the government prior to the referendum pledged that 'the Government will implement what you decide' (UK Government 2016).

SECURITY AND DEFENCE AND THE POST-REFERENDUM HANGOVER

The results of the 23rd June 2016 referendum showed 51.9% of those voted were in favour of leave the EU, while 48.1% were in favour of remain, on the basis of an overall turnout of 72.2% (implying that around 13 million did not vote) (BBC 2016). There were significant variations in the vote with majorities in Northern Ireland and Scotland voting to remain, while majorities in England and Wales voted to leave. Within a week of the referendum media reports, based on polling data, suggested that up to 7% of people who voted in the referendum now regret their choice (so-called Bregretters) (Dearden 2016). In spite of this Theresa May, who was appointed as Prime Minister following David Cameron's resignation in the immediate aftermath of the referendum, insisted that 'the people have spoken' (Riley-Smith 2016).

May's private position, laid out before a speech to Goldman Sachs, was that continued membership of the Single Market was vital but that this should not be at the expense of control over immigration, which had been the defining issue of the leave campaign. She also said that, 'There are definitely things we can do as members of the European Union that I think keep us more safe', citing the European Arrest Warrant and information-sharing between police and intelligence services (Mason 2016). May's private position serves as a useful reminder that security and defence in the European context is not only about a headline grabbing 'European army' but about intense cooperation with the EU on many aspects of internal security, including counterterrorism, cybersecurity and trafficking.

Michael Fallon, former Secretary of State for Defence, set the tone for the prospective negotiations with the EU by noting that although leaving the EU would mean that the UK would 'be working harder to commit to NATO and our key allies', it would also be in the strategic interests of the UK to continue to work with the EU on defence issues (House of Lords 2016a, 10).

In October 2016 the pound sank to a low, falling as much as 6%, to rates not seen since 1985. Some of this was ascribed to the growing economic uncertainties surrounding Brexit and considerable internal debate about whether a Brexit should be 'hard', 'soft', or inspired by Canadian, Norwegian or Swiss models. In December 2016 the EU's chief negotiator, Michel Barnier, outlined the process for the Brexit negotiations and vowed to make all EU positions transparent and available to the public. The ability of the EU to 'conclude with one or more third countries or international organisations agreements establishing an association involving reciprocal rights and obligations, common action and special procedure' is enshrined in the Lisbon Treaty (Lisbon Treaty 2009, Article 217).

In January 2017 May outlined the government's general position in a speech at Lancaster House in the form of twelve 'principles', which included 'providing certainty and clarity, taking control of our own laws' and 'strengthening the Union'—the latter being a reference to the union of England, Northern Ireland, Scotland and Wales. These principles were elaborated upon in a White Paper the following month (UK Government 2017a, 5–6). The government's White Paper on the future of the UK's relations spoke of honouring 'the choice that the people of the UK made' and that 'the people of the UK voted to leave the EU' (UK Government 2017a, 67). In the same publication the former Secretary of State for Exiting the European Union, David Davis, spoke of the need to 'respect' the wishes of the people who have voted to leave. By this time it was a moot point that referendums in the UK are advisory rather than mandatory.

The White Paper stressed that the UK is 'uniquely placed to develop and sustain a mutually beneficial model of cooperation' when it comes to counterterrorism (UK Government 2017a, Section 11.2). On broader foreign policy issues, it stressed that the 'UK will continue to be one of the most important global actors in international affairs' and that 'we want to use our tools and privileged position in international affairs to work with the EU on foreign policy security and defence' (UK Government 2017a, Section 11.9). It also mentioned the need to 'develop and sustain a mutually beneficial model of cooperation' which includes maintaining an active role in Europol, access to the Schengen II alert system (SIS II), the Advance Passenger Information and EU Passenger Name Record (PNR) data and the European Criminal Records Information System (ECRIS). On the broader issues of external security and defence the White Paper hinted at what was to come in the government's partnership paper on security and defence three months later when it noted:

Our objective is to ensure that the EU's role on defence and security is complementary to, and respects the central role of, NATO. After we leave the EU, we will remain committed to European security and add value to EU foreign and security policy. (UK Government 2017a, Section 11.11)

Also foreshadowing the partnership paper, the overall tone of the White Paper was why the EU needs the UK, with little reflection on the extent to which the UK may need the EU, especially on counterterrorism, cyber-security and information exchange.

THE WITHDRAWAL LETTER

It took almost nine months from the referendum for the UK government to deliver formal notification of withdrawal from the European Union under Article 50 of the Treaty on the Functioning of the European Union (one of the constituent parts of the Lisbon Treaty). This was done on 29 March 2017 in the form of a latter from May to Donald Tusk, the President of the European Council. The letter appeared to link the security dimension of the forthcoming negotiations with agreement in other areas, notably trade, when it stated that:

If ... we leave the European Union without an agreement the default position is that we would have to trade on the World Trade Organisation terms. In security terms a failure to reach agreement would mean our cooperation in the fight against crime and terrorism would be weakened. In this kind of scenario, both the United Kingdom and the European Union would of course cope with the change, but it is not the outcome that either side should seek. (Prime Minister's Office 2017)

The wording of the letter was widely seen as a threat by a number of EU leaders, such as Guy Verhofstadt, the European Parliament's Brexit coordinator, only to be met with vigorous denials by David Davis, Foreign Secretary Boris Johnson, and Michael Fallon who insisted that the 'UK was not seeking to blackmail the EU by threatening to withdraw security cooperation if it did not get the economic deal it wants' (Wintour et al. 2017). Even if we take this argument at face value, the type of partnership arrangements reached between the EU and the UK will inevitably be coloured by the general progress of negotiations. Indeed, it is difficult to separate them since if the UK ends up trading on WTO terms, due to either the failure of negotiations or an expiry of the (two year) Article 50 timeline, this will have important knock-on effects for the UK's defence industries, including existing and potential multi-national collaboration. It is also true that the prospect of the loss of the UK's contributions to the EU budget and the European Development Fund, which are almost 12% and 15% respectively, might lead to more EU accommodation in other fields, like security and defence, on the part of the EU negotiators. It is also possible that the UK may offset the costs of its EU divorce and revaluation of the pound against development cooperation and other residual funding obligations.

The day after the formal notification of the UK's intention to withdraw from the EU, the May government published a further White Paper with details of the Great Repeal Bill (now known as the Withdrawal Bill), by which Parliament will repeal the 1972 European Communities Act under which the UK joined the European Communities (prior to it becoming the European Union) and convert around 20,000 pieces of EU law onto the UK statute books (UK Government 2017b).[2] Under Article 50 the EU treaties applying to the UK shall cease to apply on the date of entry into force of the withdrawal agreement or, failing that, two years after formal notification (that is, 29 March 2019) (European Commission 2018).[3]

The European Council issued its guidelines for the Brexit negotiations on 29 April 2017, exactly a month after Prime Minister May triggered Article 50 and thus set the clock ticking on the UK's withdrawal from the EU. The guidelines noted that on the broader questions of security, defence and foreign policy, and other areas 'unrelated to trade', the EU stands ready to 'establish partnerships' (European Council 2017, Para. 22).

The months following the referendum in the UK saw a Cabinet reshuffle, leadership contests and, eventually, a general election on 8 June 2017 which resulted in a loss of the Conservative's majority at the expense of sizeable Labour gains. The Conservatives were forced to turn to Northern Ireland's Democratic Unionist Party (DUP) to form a new government. The Conservative Party manifesto stressed social care, education and tax

[2] This is not simply a case of transposing EU law since in many cases equivalent roles to those played by the European Commission and the European Court of Justice will have to be determined.

[3] At the time of writing the bill passed a second reading on 11 September 2017 and will now move to committee stage. Following that there will be a report stage in both Houses, followed by a third reading, prior to consideration of amendments and eventual Royal assent.

issues alongside immigration. On defence the manifesto made a pledge to not only meet NATO's target of 2% of GDP to be spent on defence, but to increase spending by 'at least half a per cent more than inflation every year' (Conservative and Unionist Party 2017, 41). The lengthy Labour Party manifesto included a section on 'Global Britain' but only at the end did it acknowledge that the UK 'will face both challenges and opportunities' as a result of Brexit (Labour Party 2017, 117). The term 'Global Britain' has since entered Brexit's political lexicon, although it remains unformulated in policy terms.

With the elections out of the way, the May government could begin negotiations with Brussels in earnest, although her mandate and authority were widely seen as weakened by her EU counterparts. The Prime Minister initially insisted in March, in her formal notice of withdrawal letter to Tusk, that 'we believe that it is necessary to agree the terms of our future partnership *alongside* those of our withdrawal from the EU' (Prime Minister's Office 2017, emphasis added). But, on the first day of the Brexit talks, when the general procedures for the ensuing negotiations were discussed, Michel Barnier made it clear that it would be a two-stage process, dependent upon satisfactory agreement on the first stage before moving to the latter (Barnier 2017a). The first part involved agreement on the UK's financial commitments to the EU (often called the 'divorce bill'), the rights of EU citizens in the UK and *vice versa*, and Northern Ireland's border with the EU. Other issues, such as any future security or trade relations, were therefore subject to making sufficient progress on the first phase. The first phase was concluded to the satisfaction of the EU27 in December 2017, but with many specifics on citizen's rights and the compatibility of a 'soft border' between Northern Ireland and the Republic of Ireland with the UK's possible withdrawal from the Single Market and Customs Union largely unspecified.

THE UK GOVERNMENT'S PARTNERSHIP PAPER AND THE EU'S GLOBAL STRATEGY

Details of the UK government's priorities and general positions vis-à-vis the negotiations began to appear slowly in the following months in the form of future partnership papers and position papers released by UK's Department for Exiting the European Union. David Davis explained that the former 'set out our thinking regarding our special partnership with the

EU' and that they differ from the latter which 'set out the position for negotiations' (Newson 2017, 2–3). Davis also added that future partnership papers are 'designed to make points to our European partners so that they could see what the future might look like under our vision' (Newson 2017, 3).

The future partnership paper on 'Foreign policy, defence and development' appeared on 12 September 2017. It was the first paper of this ilk and, as such, it was intended to set a positive tone for future papers and the ensuing negotiations (UK Government 2017c). Until this point foreign and security policy was 'the dog that is yet to bark post-Brexit' (Whitman 2016b). There were two reasons for this. First, security and defence were not priorities compared to trade or immigration questions. Second, it was widely assumed that any eventual negotiations on security and defence would be reasonably straightforward compared to many other aspects since they are largely intergovernmental—in other words, decision-making on security and defence in the EU lies principally in the hands of the Member States and security cooperation largely depends on cooperation with other EU members. This contrasts significantly with, for example, external trade where the EU has very strong and exclusive competences.

The decision to bundle together foreign policy, defence and development into one partnership paper presented its own problems. The competence issues surrounding development are different from those pertaining to security and defence. Other areas of external action, like humanitarian aid and assistance, are also addressed fleetingly in the paper and would perhaps have merited separate attention. Cooperation on development between the EU and the UK will be determined on a case-by-case basis (funds such as the Emergency Trust Fund for Africa and the EU Facility for Refugees in Turkey are mentioned in passing). Any such cooperation will evidently take place on the basis of calculations of the UK's national interests which poses awkward questions for the future of the EU's relations with the African Caribbean and Pacific (ACP) countries, as well as upon the implementation of the EU's Global Strategy and the new Consensus on Development. It also implies significant ambiguity as the EU moves towards the twelfth European Development Fund about whether the UK will contribute and, if so, how much.[4] There are therefore uncertainties in the UK's position

---

[4] The European Development Fund is not budgetised (i.e. not formally part of the EU's budget) so it is feasible that the UK could choose to align itself.

on development, more so than security and defence, which makes any in-depth analysis problematic and beyond the scope of this volume.

On security and defence specifically, the September partnership paper presented the parameters of the envisaged partnership between the UK and the EU:

- Future relations could include 'mirroring participation by other third countries contributing to European security, which offer differing levels of assets and capabilities'. But, having said this, the paper makes it clear that the UK would like a relationship that is 'deeper than any current third country partnership' (UK Government 2017c, 18);
- The UK offers the availability of UK assets, capabilities and influence to the EU and European partners in foreign, defence, cyber, development and external issues, as well as a number of cross-cutting ones;
- Regular and close consultation on foreign and security policy issues, with the option of agreeing upon joint positions on foreign policy issues, including sanctions listings, sharing information and policy alignment;
- Continued cooperation, where there are common objectives and shared threats, via existing foreign policy mechanisms, such as election monitoring missions and conflict management tools like the Early Warning System and Stabilisation Mechanisms;
- Continued close cooperation on counterterrorism and countering violent extremism;
- The opportunity to work together in CSDP missions and operations, including on mandate development and detailed operational planning;
- Greater cooperation between the EU and NATO, in line with the 2016 Joint Declaration and Implementation Plan;
- Explore how UK and European defence and security industries can continue to work together to deliver the capabilities that we need, including UK-EU collaboration on European Defence Agency (EDA) projects and initiatives and participation in the European Defence Fund (EDF), the European Defence Research Programme and the European Defence Industrial Development Programme;
- Cooperation on space (including the application of Galileo to UK and EU security);

- Collaboration on cyber security, including UK participation in the CSIRT network, the promotion of strategic frameworks for conflict prevention, cooperation and security in cyberspace;
- Alignment between the UK and EU on development policy and programming to support the UN's Sustainable Development Goals, early warning, conflict prevention and stabilisation;
- Cooperation with the EU on external migration, including the key regional frameworks and the UK's bilateral engagement with a range of source and transit countries;
- A reciprocal exchange of foreign and security policy experts and military personnel, the exchange of classified information to support external actions and the mutual provision of consular services in third countries.

The attraction of the offer from the UK perspective, which mirrored the February White Paper and foreshadowed the July 2018 White Paper, lay in the fact that 'The UK is—and will remain—a major global diplomatic, defence, development and trade policy actor' (UK Government 2017c, 6). There was, however, little apparent consideration that the UK's global role and status might be linked in part to its membership of the EU. Nevertheless, such was the confidence in the UK as a vital security partner for the EU that Crispin Blunt, who was chair of the UK Foreign Affairs Select Committee even suggested, prior to the appearance of the September partnership paper, establishing an EU equivalent of NATO's Enhanced Opportunity Partnership (EoP) (Blunt 2017).[5] The spirit of his suggestion was enthusiastically picked up by William Hague and Lord George Robertson, a former NATO Secretary-General, and more recently by Ana Palacio, a former Spanish Foreign Minister. The latter even mused that any future arrangements might entail 'the secondment of UK staff to the EU External Action Service, as well as UK participation in the European Union's powerful ambassador-level Political and Security Committee (PSC), which shapes much of the EU's foreign policy. It was also posited that the EU's counter-piracy initiative *Operation Atalanta*, off the Horn of Africa, could also keep its headquarters in the UK' (Palacio 2017).

The September 2017 partnership paper notes, 'the UK contributes people, finance, equipment or operational support to all 15 CSDP

[5] EoPs were created at the 2014 Wales Summit. Five currently exist (Australia, Finland, Georgia, Jordan and Sweden).

operations and missions' (UK Government 2017c, 10). The UK's leadership role in *Operation Atalanta*, with its Operational Headquarters at Northwood was noted, as was the presence of a naval vessel, HMS *Echo*, as part *Operation Sophia* in the Mediterranean and the presence of a 120-strong intermediate reserve company in Bosnia Herzegovina.[6] The UK's appeal for a 'deep and special partnership with the EU that goes beyond existing third country arrangements' was elucidated by Prime Minister May in her Florence speech of 22 September 2017 when she noted that 'there is no pre-existing model for co-operation between the EU and external partners which replicates the full scale and depth of the collaboration that currently exists between the EU and the UK on security, law enforcement and criminal justice' (Foreign and Commonwealth Office 2017).

But, the actual record of the UK's contributions to past and ongoing CSDP missions stands at variance with the confidence, even entitlement, portrayed in the partnership paper (Fig. 1.1). Of the 35 past or current CSDP missions the UK has contributed to 25 with an average of 15.72 personnel per mission.[7] In terms of all of the missions, the UK's personnel contributions equal 2.3% of the total contributions by the EU's members (or 4.3% of those operations and missions to which it contributed) (calculated by the author from Di Mauro et al. 2017, 97–107). When looked at over a period of time (2003–2015) the UK only provided only 110 of 12,140 EU military personnel and 209 out of 4895 civilian personnel (Bakker et al. 2016, 4). The UK's contributions pale in comparison to France who has contributed a significantly higher percentage of personnel (over 30%) compared to the other participating countries on twelve occasions. The UK has only led once in personnel contributions, in a regional maritime capacity building mission to Somalia involving 19 UK personnel, out of the 35 past or current CSDP missions or operations. A House of Lords report notes, 'the UK does not supply personnel to the missions in proportion to its population size in the EU (14.8%)' (House of Lords 2016b, 53). In comparative

---

[6] Not noted is the UK colocation, with France, of the Galileo Security Monitoring Centre which will have to be relocated.

[7] The principal UK contributions have been to CSDP operations/missions in the Mediterranean (Sophia), the police mission in Afghanistan, the regional maritime capacity building mission in Somalia, the rule of law mission in Kosovo and the EU military training mission in Mali.

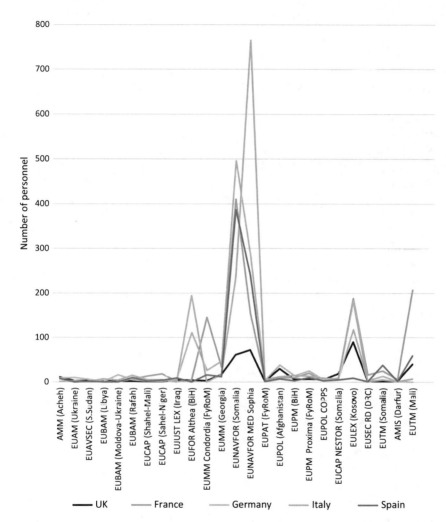

Fig. 1.1 A comparison of personnel contributions with select EU Member States in those cases where the UK contributed to CSDP missions/operations. Source: Compiled by author from information in Di Mauro et al. (2017), *EU's Global Engagement: A Database of CSDP Military Operations and Civilian Missions Worldwide*, Version 2.0 (European University Institute), pp. 45–79

terms, the UK ranks behind Austria, Romania and Turkey in terms of overall personnel contributions.

In other respects, the UK has contributed to CSDP via the 'Battlegroups' (EUBG) which consists of around 1500 troops, or a battalion, along with the relevant combat support elements. The EUBG's rotate every six months, with two on standby at any one time. The UK, along with France and Germany, proposed the concept in 2004 to ensure that the EU was in the position to deploy forces rapidly in response to a UN request. The UK was a 'Lead Nation' twice, in July-December 2013 and again in July-December 2016 with around 2330 in total involved. The UK's place on the roster to lead a Battlegroup in the second half of 2019 will obviously have to be reallocated. Each EUBG has a 'framework' or lead nation which assumes operational command and is associated with a headquarters.[8] But, the UK has not provided any funding specifically for EUBGs since 2010. The EUBG concept has met with frequent criticism throughout the EU since they have never been deployed, in spite of the fact that they reached full operational capacity in January 2007. Aside from questions of whether the size and design of EUBGs are appropriate, Brexit will remove significant forces and a 'framework' nation from the equation. It is, however, possible that the UK could continue from outside the EU, as Norway has since 2008 in the case of the Nordic Battlegroup (led by Sweden in the first half of 2015) or Ukraine in the case of the Visegrad Battlegroup (with the Czech Republic, Hungary and Poland). For balance, it should be noted that the UK is a major contributor to the 800 strong NATO battle group participating in the Enhanced Forward Presence in Estonia where the UK provides a framework battalion and a company to Poland, as part of the US-led NATO task force. The UK has of course also acted outside the CSDP framework, as in the case of the NATO-backed coalition in Libya in 2011 and that against IS in Syria and Libya.

The UK's demands for some form of unique partnership will therefore have to be weighed up against the fact that the UK has 'not chosen to put substantial forces into CSDP over the past 15 years' (House of Lords 2018) and that the UK has 'never defined [its] global outlook primarily through our membership of the European Union or by a collective European foreign policy' (UK Government 2018).

---

[8] The Concept is one that is particularly prevalent in Germany where the *Bundeswehr* has been structured as a backbone to work alongside 16 countries including Belgium, the Czech Republic, Denmark, the Netherlands, Poland and a number of non-EU militaries like Switzerland.

In contrast to the general picture of the UK's reluctance to engage significant personnel in CSDP operations, Angus Lapsley, a former UK Ambassador to the Political and Security Committee (PSC), argued that 'what we have tended to contribute has been more about leadership and broader diplomatic support' and that the UK concentrated on offering, for example, 'very high-quality staff officers, rather than putting in a lot of troops or assets, which other European Member States may well have, and our own are more usefully used elsewhere' (House of Lords 2018, 3). He is of course correct that any measure of national contributions to CSDP missions should include the qualitative aspect, but 'leadership' in the form of command of civilian operations, military missions or head of mission, are ruled out during the transition period and beyond, along with the provision of operational headquarters. The issue of where the post-Brexit operational command of Operation *Atalanta* should be located is already the subject of horse-trading between France and Spain (with the former expressing willingness to back Spain's bid for Cadiz, if Brest can host the Maritime Security Centre for the Horn of Africa, to the consternation of Italy).

Lapsley also observed that the UK accounts for around 16% of the common costs of CSDP missions and around 20% of the force catalogue (House of Lords 2018, 14). While neither should be discounted, common costs only amount to around 10–15% of the total CSDP mission costs (with the remainder being borne by the contributing EU members and third parties). The force catalogue shows those resources potentially available to the EU but there is no assumption of automatic availability, as the UK's actual contributions show.

The UK's appeal for a unique partnership with the EU was also based on invocation of the broadly shared goal of a 'safe and secure world' and threats that are increasing in 'scale, complexity and pace' (UK Government 2017c, 2). Prime Minister May's Florence speech reinforced this point by appealing to shared threats and values as the basis for a 'bold new security partnership' in the form of a treaty between the UK and EU (Foreign and Commonwealth Office 2017). May returned to the same theme again in her speech to the Munich Security Conference where she emphasized that shared values 'have created common cause to act together in our common interest' (UK Government 2018). There is, at least at face value, no disputing that the EU and the UK share the same values, as laid out in the Lisbon Treaty.[9] These values are, however, not unique to the EU. The

---

[9] Notably the Treaty on European Union, Articles 3 and 21.

North Atlantic Treaty of 4 April 1949, establishing NATO, also makes the appropriate normative references in its preamble which includes a reaffirmation of the faith of the signatories in the 'purposes and principles of the Charter of the United Nations' (NATO 1949, Preamble). A joint EU-NATO declaration issued in July 2016 also makes reference to the shared values of the membership of the two organisations (NATO 2016). Thus, although any post-Brexit arrangements will continue to be based on broadly similar world outlooks and shared values, any appeal for some kind of special status based upon normative grounds is hard to accept when, for instance, Canada or Norway would have equal claim.

Similar arguments are applied to threat perceptions when it is argued that the 'UK and EU citizens face the same threats' (UK Government 2017c, 2). The threats laid out in the UK's 2015 Strategic Defence and Security Review (SDSR) are mirrored in the EU's Global Strategy, adopted the following year. These are summarised in the former as (UK Government 2015, 15):

- The increasing threat posed by terrorism, extremism and instability.
- The resurgence of state-based threats; and intensifying wider state competition.
- The impact of technology, especially cyber threats; and wider technological developments.
- The erosion of the rules-based international order, making it harder to build consensus and tackle global threats.

The EU Global Strategy notes that the threats facing the EU have 'both an internal and an external dimension' and they include 'terrorism, hybrid threats, cyber and energy security, organised crime and external border management' (EU Global Strategy 2016, 20). In spite of the shared values and threat perceptions, it is striking how little the EU actually appears in the SDSR. The UK's SDSR mentions CSDP twice and, in both instances, *en passant*. This is also borne out in the Foreign and Commonwealth Office's 2016 Single Departmental Plan where, in pre-referendum mode, the EU is seen as occasionally useful for the advancement of UK objectives, but it was more commonly seen in the context of Prime Minster David Cameron's renegotiation agenda (stressing competitiveness, economic governance, sovereignty and welfare/migration). More often than not, the UK's role is portrayed as one of nudging or cajoling the EU towards policies or agreements that the UK wishes to promote (such as an ambitious EU Trade Strategy focussing on further deals of importance to the UK such as with Australia and New Zealand, continued sanctions on Russia, maintaining observance of the Joint Comprehensive Plan of Action and developing the European Neighbourhood Policy) (Foreign and Commonwealth Office 2016). Moreover, the emphasis on the strong commonalities between the EU and UK sits rather uncomfortably with the underpinning logic of the Brexit process and the desire to be a 'global, free-trading nation, able to chart our own way in the world' (Foreign and Commonwealth Office 2017).

In addition to complementarities, the strategic-level documents also betray interesting differences. The UK's SDSR is unabashedly built around the projection of 'global influence' to 'protect and promote our interests and values, supporting our security and prosperity' (UK Government 2015, 47). The EU's 'Global Strategy' (EUGS) also has universal aspirations, but a careful reading shows that the EU's strategic priorities lie in the European neighbourhood to the east and the south. The EU's global interests are primarily in trade and development while its ability to exert foreign and, most notably, security and defence influence at the global level is limited. Whether the UK really is a global actor is open to dispute, but its diplomatic weight, trade links, other forms of 'soft power' (especially its cultural influence) and harder power assets (the UK still maintains modest basing access in locations outside Europe) make it a plausible claim.

When it comes to CSDP, the EUGS is adamant that:

> While NATO exists to defend its members—most of which are European—from external attack, Europeans must be better equipped, trained and organised to contribute decisively to such collective efforts, as well as to act autonomously if and when necessary. An appropriate level of ambition and strategic autonomy is important for Europe's ability to foster peace and safeguard security within and beyond its borders. (EU Global Strategy 2016, 19)

The precise nature of any 'autonomy' is unclear and poses broader questions about the EU's ultimate level of ambition, its relations with NATO and the degree of desirable dependence on the US. This formulation is an echo of an earlier document agreed to between Prime Minister Tony Blair and President Jacques Chirac in 1998 which also made reference to the 'capacity for autonomous action' (St Malo Declaration 1998, Para. 2). In both instances it is clear that the EU wishes to work with partners, but that it should also develop the capabilities for independent action which raises the issue of where the UK fits in the Union's ambition for strategic autonomy.

The comparison of EU and national level strategic documents is of course open to the objection that the latter are bound to promote national interests and rightly so. The Foreign and Commonwealth Office's Single Departmental Plan is clearly designed to impress upon its paymasters that it delivers value for money for the UK. Nevertheless, the various national position and strategy papers, when compared to the government's 'Future Partnership Paper' pose some awkward questions.

Overall, there is little pre-referendum evidence that the EU was central to UK foreign or security policy. The EU is certainly mentioned, but often as part of wider multilateral relations with other organisations (like NATO or the UN) and rarely in the context of the strengthening of the UK's key bilateral relations, most notably with the United States. The track record of pro-activism, stressed in the partnership paper, contrasts with the sometimes-obstructive role that the UK has played in the EU's foreign and security policy. The desire for a 'deep and special partnership' has to be contrasted with two British-inspired declarations that are attached to the Lisbon Treaty. Both served to remind the EU that the provisions covering CFSP, the advent of the new High Representative/Vice-President and the External Action Service, 'will not affect the existing legal basis, responsibilities, and powers of each Member State in relation to the formulation and conduct of its foreign policy, its national diplomatic service, relations with third countries and participation in international organisations, including a Member State's membership of the Security Council of the United Nations' (Lisbon Treaty 2009, Declaration 14). As Barnier (2017b) acerbically noted, the partnership paper was a 'rare statement in support of European defence policy'.

Conclusions

The picture that emerges is of a country where the EU was *not* of great importance to the UK's strategic objectives, its diplomacy and foreign engagement or to its security and defence, with the important exception of some areas pertaining directly to the UK's national security. On matters of security and defence, as Richard Whitman has argued, the UK shifted from being a leader in the late 1990s to a 'laggard in recent years. London has not been willing to engage at a significant level with CSDP military operations. Further, it has been resistant to proposals to further deepen defence integration among EU member states' (Whitman 2016b). Such opinions sit awkwardly with the UK's quest for the deep and special partnership with the EU of the type envisaged in the September paper, especially if based on an assessment of the UK's engagement with the EU on foreign and security policies over the years. It can, for instance, be questioned whether the 150 UK personnel committed to EU missions and operations really is, as Michael Fallon put it, a demonstration of 'Britain's global reach' (Fallon 2017). It also calls into question the claim made by Prime Minister May that the UK is 'working ever more closely with our European partners, bringing the influence and impact that comes from our full range of global relationships' (UK Government 2018). This is only partially true.

As the UK dithered and prevaricated over its post-Brexit role the EU moved ahead with formulating and implementing its own strategic interests and in rapidly developing security and defence plans. For the EU Brexit represented a window of opportunity. The High Representative/Vice-President (HR/VP), Federica Mogherini, made this plain in a speech to the assembled EU Heads of Delegation (Ambassadors) in Brussels, when she reminded them that 'we have the political space today to do things that were not really do-able in the previous years' (Mogherini 2016). Although there is evident regret from the EU27 regarding the outcome of the 'sovereign choice made by the British', it also represented a chance to move towards a 'Europe of Defence' (Barnier 2017b). The distance between the EU and the UK's post-Brexit security aspirations may widen even further due to the feeling that the EU now has, as Commission President Jean-Claude Juncker, put it, 'wind in our sails' (European Commission 2017).

REFERENCES

Associated Press. (2016, May 25). Former Military Officers Join Brexit Campaign. *The Guardian*. Retrieved from https://www.theguardian.com/politics/2016/may/25/more-former-military-officers-join-brexit-campaign-eu-referendum.

Bakker, A., Drent, M., & Zandee, D. (2016, July). *European Defence: How to Engage the UK After Brexit*. Clingendael Report.

Barnier, M. (2017a, June 19). *Speech by Michel Barnier, the European Commission's Chief Negotiator, Following the First Round of Article 50 Negotiations with the UK*. Speech 17/1704, Brussels.

Barnier, M. (2017b, November 29). *Speech by Michel Barnier at the Berlin Security Conference*. SPEECH/17/5021, Berlin.

BBC. (2016). *EU Referendum Results*. Retrieved from http://www.bbc.com/news/politics/eu_referendum/results.

Blunt, C. (2017). *Post-Brexit EU-UK Cooperation on Foreign and Security Policy*. Retrieved from https://www.blunt4reigate.com/sites/www.blunt4reigate.com/files/2017-04/Post-Brexit%20EU-UK%20cooperation%20on%20foreign%20%26%20security%20policy%20April%202017.pdf.

Britain Stronger in Europe. (2015). *Britain's Place in the World*. Retrieved from http://www.strongerin.co.uk/get_the_facts#hDa080RbPfdHoT18.97.

Cameron, D. (2015, November 10). *A New Settlement for the United Kingdom in a Reformed European Union*. Letter from Prime Minister Cameron to Donald Tusk, President of the European Council.

Cameron, D. (2016, May 9). *PM Speech on UK's Strength and Security in the EU*. Retrieved from https://www.gov.uk/government/speeches/pm-speech-on-the-uks-strength-and-security-in-the-eu-9-may-2016.

Clarke, K. (2015, October 11). Pro-Europeans Must Make an Optimistic Case for Staying. *The Independent*.

Conservative and Unionist Party. (2017). *Forward Together: Our Plan for a Stronger Britain and a Prosperous Future*.

Dearden, L. (2016, July 1). Brexit Research Suggests That 1.2 Million Leave Voters Regret Their Choice in Reversal That Could Change Result. *The Independent*.

Dearlove, R. (2016, March 23). Brexit Would Not Damage UK Security. *Prospect*. Retrieved from http://www.prospectmagazine.co.uk/opinions/brexit-would-not-damage-uk-security.

Deutsche Welle. (2015, March 8). Juncker Calls for Collective EU Army. *Deutsche Welle*. Retrieved from http://www.dw.com/en/juncker-calls-for-collective-eu-army/a-18302459.

Di Mauro, D., Krotz, U., & Wright, K. (2017). *EU's Global Engagement: A Database of CSDP Military Operations and Civilian Missions Worldwide*. Version 2.0 (European University Institute), pp. 97–107.

EU Global Strategy. (2016, June). *Shared Vision, Common Action: A Stronger Europe. A Global Strategy for the European Union's Foreign and Security Policy*.

European Commission. (2017, September 13). *President Jean-Claude Juncker's State of the Union Address 2017*. Brussels.

European Commission. (2018, February 28). *European Commission Draft Withdrawal Agreement on the Withdrawal of the United Kingdom of Great Britain and Northern Ireland from the European Union and the European Atomic Energy Community*. TF50 (2018) 33.

European Council. (2017). *Guidelines for Brexit Negotiations Following the UK's Notification Under Article 50 TEU*. Press Release 220/17.

Fallon, M. (2016, September 27). UK Will Oppose Plans for EU Army. *BBC News*. Retrieved from http://www.bbc.com/news/uk-politics-37482942.
Fallon, M. (2017, March 6). *Defence Secretary Underlines UK Commitment to European Security*. Retrieved from https://www.gov.uk/government/news/defence-secretary-underlines-uk-commitment-to-european-security.
Financial Times. (2016). *Poll of Polls*. Updated 23 June. Retrieved from https://ig.ft.com/sites/brexit-polling/.
Foreign and Commonwealth Office. (2016, February 19). *Corporate Report: Single Departmental Plan: 2015 to 2020*. Retrieved from https://www.gov.uk/government/publications/fco-single-departmental-plan-2015-to-2020/single-departmental-plan-2015-to-2020.
Foreign and Commonwealth Office. (2017, September 22). *A New Era of Cooperation and Partnership Between the UK and the EU*. Speech by Prime Minister Theresa May, Florence. Retrieved from https://www.gov.uk/government/speeches/pms-florence-speech-a-new-era-of-cooperation-and-partnership-between-the-uk-and-the-eu.
George, S. (1997). *An Awkward Partner: Britain in the European Community* (3rd ed.). Oxford: Oxford University Press.
House of Commons. (2016, April 19). *Implications of the Referendum on EU Membership for the UK's Role in the World*. Foreign Affairs Committee, Fifth Report of Session 2015–2016.
House of Lords. (2016a, October 13). *Library Note*. LLN 2016/051.
House of Lords. (2016b, February 16). *Europe in the World: Towards a More Effective EU Foreign and Security Strategy*. 8th Report, HL Paper 97.
House of Lords. (2018, January 11). *Oral Evidence of Angus Lapsley on Brexit: CSDP Missions, Select Committee on the European Union*. External Affairs Sub-Committee.
Labour Party. (2017). *For the Many Not the Few: Labour Party Manifesto 2017*.
Lisbon Treaty. (2009). *Treaty on the Functioning of the European Union*.
Mance, H. (2016, June 3). Britain Has Had Enough of Experts, Says Gove. *Financial Times*.
Mance, H. (2018, March 12). Global Britain Strategy Risks Damaging UK Reputation. *Financial Times*.
Mason, R. (2016, October 26). Leaked Recordings Shows Theresa May Is "Ignoring Her Own Warnings" on Brexit. *The Guardian*.
Mogherini, F. (2016, September 5). *Opening Remarks by High Representative/Vice-President Federica Mogherini at the EU Ambassador's Conference 'Shared Vision, Common Action: A Stronger Europe'*. Retrieved from https://europa.eu/globalstrategy/en/speech-hrvp-mogherini-eu-ambassadors.
NATO. (1949, April 4). *The North Atlantic Treaty*. Washington, DC. Retrieved from https://www.nato.int/cps/en/natohq/official_texts_17120.htm.

NATO. (2016, July 8). *Joint Declaration by the President of the European Council, the President of the European Commission and the Secretary-General of the North Atlantic Treaty Organization.* Press Release (2016) 119, Warsaw.

Newson, N. (2017, September 7). Position Papers and Future Partnership Papers on the UK's Future Relationship with the EU. *Library Briefing.* House of Lords.

Palacio, A. (2017, July 19). Britain's European Ties That Bind. *Project Syndicate.* Retrieved from https://www.project-syndicate.org/commentary/brexit-talks-security-defense-foreign-policy-by-ana-palacio-2017-07.

Prime Minister's Office. (2017). *Prime Minister's Letter to Donald Tusk Triggering Article 50.* Department for Exiting the European Union. Retrieved from https://www.gov.uk/government/publications/prime-ministers-letter-to-donald-tusk-triggering-article-50.

Riley-Smith, B. (2016, November 5). The People Have Made Their Democratic Decision and a Principle Is at Stake, Theresa May Tells Brexit Critics as She Vows to Battle Courts. *Daily Telegraph.*

Robertson, N. (2016, June 21). Safer In or Out of the EU? Why Security Is Key to Brexit Vote. *CNN.* Retrieved from http://edition.cnn.com/2016/06/21/europe/brexit-security-debate-robertson/index.html.

St. Malo Declaration. (1998, December 3–4). *Joint Declaration Issued at the British-French Summit, Saint Malo.* France.

UK Government. (2013, July). *Review of the Balance of Competences Between the United Kingdom and the European Union: Foreign Policy.*

UK Government. (2015). *National Security Strategy and Strategic Defence and Security Review 2015: A Secure and Prosperous United Kingdom.* Cm 9161.

UK Government. (2016, June 23). *Why the Government Believes That Voting to Remain in the European Union Is the Best Decision for the UK: The EU Referendum.*

UK Government. (2017a, February). *The United Kingdom's Exit from, and New Partnership with, the European Union: Policy Paper.* Department for Exiting the European Union.

UK Government. (2017b, March). *Legislating for the United Kingdom's Withdrawal from the European Union.* Department for Exiting the European Union, Cm 9446.

UK Government. (2017c, September 12). *Foreign Policy, Defence and Development: A Future Partnership Paper.*

UK Government. (2018, February 17). *Prime Minister Speech at the Munich Security Conference.* Retrieved from https://www.gov.uk/government/speeches/pm-speech-at-munich-security-conference-17-february-2018.

Vote Leave. (2015). *Being in the EU Undermines Our Defence.* Retrieved from http://www.voteleavetakecontrol.org/briefing_defence.html.

Whitman, R. (2016a, May). The UK's Foreign and Security Policy: What's at Stake in the Referendum? *Security Policy Brief*, Egmont Institute, Brussels, No. 73.

Whitman, R. (2016b, December 28). Brexit – Six Months On: Foreign, Security and Defence Policy. *The UK in a Changing Europe*. Retrieved from http:// ukandeu.ac.uk/brexit-six-months-on-foreign-security-and-defence-policy/.

Wintour, P., Boffey, D., & Stewart, H. (2017, March 31). Boris Johnson Joins UK Attempt to Calm Brexit Security Concerns. *The Guardian*.

CHAPTER 2

The Pre- and Post-Brexit Evolution of the EU's Common Security and Defence Policy

The extraordinary flurry of activity in the latter half of 2016 on EU security and defence may have been facilitated by the referendum result, but it was not because of it. Many of the initiatives that appeared in 2015–2016 had more to do with changes in the general strategic environment, as well as an existential crisis within the Union about its direction and purpose. Contrary to the more optimistic note of the 2003 European Security Strategy, which started by observing that, 'Europe has never been so prosperous, so secure nor so free', the EU Global Strategy (2016) commenced by noting that, 'The purpose, even existence, of our Union is being questioned' (European Security Strategy 2003, 3). Mogherini's July 2015 Strategic Review, which formed the underpinning assessment of international relations for the ensuing Global Strategy, noted the challenges stemming from a world that is more 'connected, contested and complex' (Strategic Review 2015). The security environment was portrayed as 'volatile, complex and uncertain', with Europe facing an 'arch of instability' to its east and south and, against this backdrop, it argued that 'security and defence should remain at the very centre of the European agenda' (Strategic Review 2015, 5). In order to meet these challenges and to exploit opportunities the EU needed to be able to link-up the different components of its soft power with the hard(er) aspects in what was became known as the 'joined-up' approach.

The security and defence component of this 'joined-up' approach had hitherto been weak for three reasons. The first is that the security and

© The Author(s) 2019
S. Duke, *Will Brexit Damage our Security and Defence?*,
https://doi.org/10.1007/978-3-319-96107-1_2

defence aspects of the EU have only been developed fairly recently and are scarcely a decade and a half old. When compared to development or trade, which date back to the original European Communities, these aspects remain fairly immature. Second, for much of the Cold War decisions pertaining to security and defence were taken by the respective superpowers and their military alliances. It is only a slight exaggeration to claim that the European Community, and then the EU in its early years, largely developed in a security vacuum. Third, the question of the extent to which the EU should develop its security and defence potential and how autonomous any such capabilities should be, was largely obviated until recently by the assumption that the US would underpin the security of its NATO allies, most of whom are also EU members.

Following in the footsteps of Mogherini's Strategic Review the idea of a 'European Defence Union' was advocated by the European People's Party (EPP) in November 2015 (European People's Party 2015). The paper enunciated a number of themes that were to reappear over the next year or so, such as its support for the Lisbon Treaty's start-up fund (Article 41 TEU), entrusting of a mission to a group of Member States (Article 44 TEU) and Permanent Structured Cooperation (PESCO) (Article 46 TEU). As the largest political grouping in the European Parliament, the EPP's position paper set the tone for many of the post-Brexit referendum security and defence debates. Of note with regard to these debates was the EPP's recognition of the fact that not all EU members will wish to move at the same speed or are capable of it. The EPP identified the 'lack of political will to fully use all the existing military capabilities and instruments' as a primary concern (European People's Party 2015, 5). Hence, the idea of activating the hitherto unused articles of the Lisbon Treaty, notably PESCO and the 'collective self-defence clause', were to the fore (European People's Party 2015, 23). Many of the recommendations made in the paper were echoed in the subsequent positions of France, Germany and Italy. Post-Brexit referendum proposals reiterated key parts of the EPP's position paper, such as the creation of a new EU operations headquarters, known as the Military Planning and Conduct Capability (MPCC), alongside a series of initiatives designed to increase and harmonize the capabilities of the EU's members.

One important development, when comparing the pre- and post-Brexit referendum proposals for security and defence, was the appearance of the EUGS and its strong advocacy that 'the EU needs to be strengthened as a security community' if it is to be a 'credible Union' (Strategic Review

2015, 20). Unfortunately the launch of the strategy took place only five days after the June 2016 UK referendum and was scarcely noticed amongst the post-referendum media hullabaloo. It is, however, an important document since it provided the jumping-off point, alongside the EPP position paper, for a series of national initiatives. French Foreign Minister Jean-Marc Ayrault and Federal Foreign Minister Frank-Walter Steinmeier (2016) spoke of their 'regret' at the outcome of the UK referendum and acknowledged the more general decline in support for the European project. But, both stressed their belief that 'France and Germany recognise their responsibility to reinforce solidarity and cohesion within the European Union'. As part of this Franco-German 'recommitment' to a shared vision of Europe as a security union, both advocated the formation of a European Security Compact encompassing 'all aspects of security and defence dealt with at the European level' (Ayrault and Steinmeier 2016). This was followed three months later by a joint proposal from Germany's Defence Minister, Ursula von der Leyen, and her French counterpart, Jean Yves Le Drian in September 2016 where they also concluded that, 'The defence of European countries matters for the protection of EU citizens and the credibility of the European Union as a whole' and that the EU has 'the unique ability to use and combine military and civilian instruments' (von der Leyen and le Drian 2016). In structural terms they proposed that the European Council should meet once per annum as a European Security Council which, in turn, should be prepared by a meeting of the Foreign Affairs, Defence and Interior ministers. They also advocated the creation of a permanent MPCC, a European Medical Command and a possible European logistics hub, common financing arrangements and strengthening the Eurocorps.

The push for a 're-launch' of European defence received a further boost at a Franco-German-Italian summit at Ventotene in August 2016 (which was symbolically important due to the 1944 manifesto bearing its name which urged the formation of a federation of European states) hosted by the Italian Prime Minister and the issuance of a joint statement by the three foreign ministers. The Italian Foreign Minister, Paolo Gentiloni, called for a 'Schengen for Defense' with, at its heart, 'a core group of EU countries' who can 'accelerate their integration in the area of defense, leaving others the option to join at a later state through an inclusive exercise' (Gentiloni 2016). The respective defence ministers shared the ambition to realize a 'union for European defence' but preserved the spirit of the Italian proposal in the sense that not all would be obliged to move at the same speed but those that are like-minded should be able to do so (although, rather than an *ad hoc* mechanism that Italy envisaged, it should be via PESCO) (Marrone and Camporini 2016). Shortly before a meeting of the Heads of State and Government (the European Council) Jean-Claude Juncker supported the push for a 'single headquarters' for EU operations and advocated moving towards 'common military assets, in some cases owned by the EU' and for the creation of a 'European Defence Fund' (Juncker 2016).

A New Level of Ambition

A declaration issued following an informal European Council in Bratislava in September 2016 pointed toward a new level of ambition in European security and defence and declared that, 'Although one country has decided to leave, the EU remains indispensable for the rest of us' (European Council 2016a). The informal meeting marked the 'beginning of a process', complete with a 'road map' or Implementing Plan on Security and Defence (IPSD), with the aim of rounding off the process by March 2017, symbolically marking the 60th anniversary of the Rome Treaty. The new 'level of ambition' aimed to 'tackle today's threats and challenges more effectively, with the right capabilities, tools and structures to deliver more security for its citizens' (Council of the EU 2016a, 2).

The perennial issue of capabilities was addressed in the European Commission's European Defence Action Plan (EDAP) which appeared in November 2016. EDAP's overall goal is to ensure that 'the European defence industrial base is able to meet Europe's current and future security needs and, in that respect, enhances the Union's strategic autonomy, strengthening its ability to act with partners' (European Commission 2016, 3). This is to be attained by a combination of investment in new technologies, through joint research and development wherever possible, by buttressing the European defence industrial base, avoiding duplication, as well as by various forms of sharing of platforms and assets at a time of stagnant or negative growth rates in defence expenditure.

To support these objectives the Commission proposed the launch of a European Defence Fund (EDF) to foster investment in defence supply chains and to reinforce the single market for defence. The EDF consists of a 'research window', to fund collaborative defence research projects, and a 'capability window' to support the joint development of defence capabilities to be finance by the pooling of national contributions and, where possible, supported by the EU budget. The EDF only formally came into existence in June 2017 with a research fund of €90 million allocated for 2017–2020 and €500 million per annum after 2020 and €500 million allocated for 2019–2020 and €1 billion per annum after 2020 for development and acquisition (with a leverage effect from national financing that is expected to increase this to €5 billion per annum after 2020) (European Commission 2017). It is, however, far from clear where the budget for EDF (amounting to around 1% of the total EU budget) will come from in the current financial perspective which expires in 2020, especially at a time when Brexit could imply an overall decrease of around 12% in the Union's funding for the next seven-year multiannual financial framework (MFF) when compared to the current one.

The third aspect of the development of European security and defence in the latter half of 2016 was the implementation of the Joint Declaration on EU-NATO cooperation of 8 July. The declaration, issued by the Presidents of the European Council and European Commission, as well as NATO's Secretary-General, was designed to 'give new impetus and new substance to the NATO-EU strategic partnership' (Joint Declaration 2016). The implementation plan for the Joint Declaration appeared on 6 December and included a number of specific proposals to counter hybrid threats, enhance situational awareness and strategic communication, bolstering resilience and crisis response as well as cooperation on maritime security, cyber security and defence, defence industry and research and exercises (Council of the EU 2016b). The European Council subsequently endorsed all three initiatives on 15 December 2016 and urged action on all 'in order to strengthen Europe's security and defence in a challenging geopolitical environment and to better protect its citizens' (European Council 2016b, 3).

By March 2017 the Council (i.e. foreign ministers from the EU's Member States) had endorsed the creation of a MPCC to be responsible for the 'operational planning and conduct of non-executive military missions' (EU Union 2017a). The modest 25 strong MPCC was established on 8 June 2017 but it is important to stress that this was not the full operational headquarters that had been envisaged over a decade ago by some of the EU's members since, for the time being, it is restricted to 'non-executive' missions (i.e. training missions in Somalia, Central Africa and Mali).

The March Council also applauded the initial work to launch the Coordinated Annual Review on Defence (CARD) since the current national review mechanisms allow for no overarching or systematic oversight of capabilities, shortfalls and defence spending plans. By enabling voluntary transparency at the national level, CARD could in principle strengthen EDAP, with the ambition to establish CARD on a trial basis by the end of 2017 with the aim of full implementation by 2019. But CARD's voluntary nature and the fact that it will provide an overview that is already available for NATO members, via its defence planning process (DPP), raises questions about the value-added of the initiative. Other voluntary initiatives, such as the four defence benchmarks run by the EDA since 2007 have seen, at a generous estimate, fulfilment of one of the four collective benchmarks (see Fiott 2017).

The Centrality of Permanently Structured Cooperation

The centrality of PESCO to the earlier Franco-German initiatives and the emerging plans to enhance European security and defence still left critical questions open regarding who would bear the brunt for attaining the new level of ambition. Twenty-three EU members initially expressed their intention to participate in PESCO in the margins of the November 2017 Foreign Affairs Council and they were soon joined by two more members (Fig. 2.1).[1] The agreement, which promoted a German-backed 'inclusive PESCO', rather than the French preference for a more ambitious version with higher but selective entry criteria, offered a 'reliable and binding legal framework within the EU institutional framework', where progress is subject to annual regular assessment by the High Representative (Council of the EU 2017b, 1).

The commitment to PESCO made by 25 of the EU's members included 'successive medium-term increases in defence investment expenditure to 20% of total defence spending' to increase 'the share of expenditure allocated to defence research and technology with a view to nearing the 2% of total defence spending' (Council of the EU 2017b, Annex II, 3). The key word is obviously 'nearing' since if applied as a strict condition for PESCO from the outset most, including France and Germany, would not be currently eligible for PESCO. The agreement therefore relaxes the criteria for PESCO and puts the emphasis upon commitments once pledged and the processes to attain the shared goals. Any commitments, however, will be

---

[1] Denmark, Ireland, Malta, Portugal and the UK did not initially sign, but Ireland and Portugal joined soon thereafter.

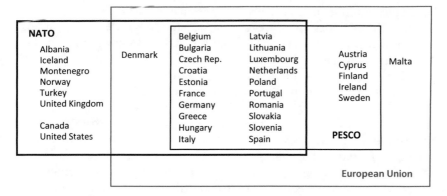

Fig. 2.1 Post Brexit EU-NATO membership including PESCO. Source: Compiled by author

hard to enforce since the timetable for achieving pledges is unclear, as is the link to the CARD process which, intuitively, should have been a prerequisite for PESCO, but which is not.

There is also the question of whether third-party participation in PESCO, with the UK in mind, could include a role in the governance structures, most notably the ministerial-level Council where Foreign and Defence ministers (usually twice per year) take decisions or adopt new projects. Project scrutiny is then carried out at various civilian and military levels, including the PSC and the EU Military Staff, as well as the EDA, facilitated by a PESCO Secretariat. In spite of the many fudges and ambiguities present in the agreement, PESCO is seen as 'an ambitious, binding and inclusive European legal framework for investments in the security and defence of the EU's territory and its citizens' (Council of the EU 2017b, Annex I, 1). It is therefore difficult to see how a non-EU state, such as post-Brexit UK, could enter into such a framework open only to members. This does not, however, exclude the possibility of UK inclusion in individual projects on an invitational basis, as confirmed by the Council meeting in PESCO format. The UK government supported PESCO's launch and views, and has suggested a cooperative accord via the EDA that would cover capability collaboration with PESCO and the EDF (UK Government 2018, 67). Any such administrative agreement with the EDA would involve some form of 'observer' status (which would have to be extended to Norway, Serbia, Switzerland and Ukraine) and a number of binding commitments. These would, presumably, involve the UK's committal to the priorities of the EU Global Strategy and to PESCO's binding commitments on, for instance, defence budgets and joint use of existing defence capabilities.The EDF may be the most challenging part since this would involve UK's acceptance of the EU's rules on defence markets and intellectual property rights, as well as a dispute resolution mechanism involving the European Court of Justice. Access to the EDF will also involve a financial commitment by the UK (logic suggests that one financial contribution covering the EDA, PESCO and EDF would be the most practical). In return the UK could bargain for a non-voting role in the EDF committees and guarantees that it (like other third states) can bid for projects on an equal basis in order to contribute to the development of EU defence capabilities.

It is of course easy to dismiss the various initiatives described above as elitist in nature. This would, however, be wrong since there has been consistent support for a common defence and security policy among the Member States during 2016–2017 (75% in favour and only 18–19% against) (Eurobarometer 2017a, 31). Interestingly, 59% of those surveyed in the UK supported a common defence and security policy and 24% were against (Eurobarometer 2017b, 3). More were in favour of a common defence and security policy in France (with 78% in favour and 16% against) and Germany (with 85% in favour and 12% against). But, more were opposed to the notion in Austria (with 36% against) than the UK, with many other sharing the UK's scepticism (like the Czech Republic, Finland, Ireland, Greece, Hungary and Italy). What makes the UK figures stand out is the relatively high number of 'don't knows' (at 17% compared to the EU28 average of 7%). Care has to be obviously taken not to over-interpret such public opinion data, but it does at least indicate that a majority of those surveyed in the UK were not opposed to a common security and defence policy, even after the June 2016 referendum results. It also suggests that there is strong support across the EU and that, aside from free movement of EU citizens, a common defence and security policy enjoys the highest support compared to many other policy areas (like migration, energy, foreign policy, monetary union or enlargement).

The success of PESCO and European defence more generally will depend heavily upon Franco-German alignment and cooperation. Given the French preference for a more select initial approach to PESCO stressing capabilities, it remains to be seen whether President Macron's

European Intervention Initiative (EII) will emerge as a complement or alternative to PESCO outside the EU. It is quite possible that EII could offer a complementary approach to PESCO, but if the latter falters for any reason, the onus will then fall on developing the capacity to act outside the EU. In this event, the Anglo-French coupling that led to CSDP may once again become vital to guaranteeing Europe's security and defence, but this time from outside the Union.

Britain's often ambivalent attitude towards EU security and defence has facilitated security and defence development at the EU level which, as the High Representative maintains, 'is not a plan anymore, it is not a dream anymore, it is reality coming true' (Mogherini 2017). The creation of the MPCC, the possibility of a larger budget for the EDA and the reform of the Athena mechanism (covering some of the common costs of EU operations and missions like headquarters, administration, infrastructure and medical services) would predictably have been resisted by the UK. Ironically, the reform of Athena may prove of some interest to the UK in terms of either its participation in CSDP military operations, or even the provision of a Battlegroup, since it has been proposed that 'the deployment of Battlegroups should be borne as a common cost by the EU-managed Athena mechanism' (European Council 2017, 5).[2] The Athena mechanism applies with equal validity both to EU members participating as well as to third countries. Athena's attraction should not, however, be overstated since the current mechanism covers around 10–15% of the costs of an operation, the remaining costs being borne by those contributing on a 'costs fall where they lie' principle (European Parliament 2016, 2). The UK could therefore still end up making potentially significant contributions to any EU military operation it becomes involved in.

Conclusions

To summarise this section, security and defence came to the fore of the EU's agenda to initially overcome the challenges present in a rapidly changing world and, latterly, to respond to an existential crisis. Security and defence emerged as a rather unlikely candidate to reinvigorate enthusiasm in the European project, but it was one that echoed the insecurities in the EU arising from Russia's military build-up on the EU's eastern

[2] The UK will be obliged to continue the financing of common costs (Athena) during any transition period.

borders as well as acts of terrorism in Belgium, France, Germany and elsewhere which added to an atmosphere of threat and insecurity. The UK's June 2016 referendum results may have added fuel to a pre-existing existential crisis in the EU, but it also opened the political space for progress in policy areas where the UK had often been unenthusiastic or even obstructive. It was therefore symbolically important that a year after the referendum and the appearance of the EUGS the High Representative, Federica Mogherini, was able to announce that on security and defence 'more has been achieved in the last ten months than in the last ten years' (EU Global Strategy 2017, 5).

The exact amount of progress towards what may become a European Defence Union can be debated since most of the results so far are at the political level and have yet to be translated into real cooperation and capabilities. Even so, the progress Mogherini referred to is also a measure of the political and aspirational gulf that has developed between the EU's members and the UK. Any desire to involve the UK from the EU side in its security and defence will be tempered by the knowledge that they are in part where they are because of the absence, not presence, of the UK. The flurry of activity since 2016, even if still largely on paper, is indicative of the EU's determination to formulate its own security and defence policies without the UK if necessary from 29 March 2019. The EU should be open to flexible arrangements with the UK on collaboration with the EDA, PESCO and EDF in the form of an administrative agreement that would enable British participation, but this will come at a price and with political and legal commitments.

REFERENCES

Ayrault, J.-M., & Steinmeier, F.-W. (2016, June 27). *Joint Contribution by Foreign Ministers Jean-Marc Ayrault and Frank-Walter Steinmeier, A Strong Europe in a World of Uncertainties.* Retrieved from https://www.auswaertiges-amt.de/en/aussenpolitik/europa/160624-bm-am-fra-st/281702.

Council of the EU. (2016a, November 14). *Implementation Plan on Security and Defence.* 14392/16, Brussels.

Council of the EU. (2016b, December 6). *Council Conclusions on the Implementation of the Joint Declaration by the President of the European Council, the President of the European Commission and the Secretary General of the North Atlantic Treaty Organization.* 15283/16, Brussels.

Council of the EU. (2017a). *Council Conclusions on Progress in Implementing the EU.*

Council of the EU. (2017b, November 13). *Notification on Permanent Structured Cooperation to the Council and to the High Representative of the Union for Foreign Affairs and Security Policy.* Annex 1: Principles of PESCO.

EU Global Strategy. (2016, June). *Shared Vision, Common Action: A Stronger Europe. A Global Strategy for the European Union's Foreign and Security Policy.*

EU Global Strategy. (2017, June). *From Shared Vision to Common Action: Implementing the EU Global Strategy, Year 1.*

Eurobarometer. (2017a). *Public Opinion in the European Union: Standard Eurobarometer 87.* First Results, Spring.

Eurobarometer. (2017b). *Standard Barometer 87: The Key Indicators.* Spring 2017.

European Commission. (2016, November 30). *Communication from the Commission to the European Parliament, the European Council, the Council, the European Economic and Social Committee and the Committee of the Regions, European Defence Action Plan.* COM (2016) 950 Final, Brussels.

European Commission. (2017, June 7). *A European Defence Fund: €5.5 Billion Per Year to Boost Europe's Defence Capabilities.* IP/17/1508, Brussels.

European Council. (2016a, September 16). *The Bratislava Declaration.*

European Council. (2016b, December 15). *European Council Conclusions.* EUCO34/16, Brussels.

European Council. (2017, 22 June). *European Council Conclusions on Security and Defence.* Press Release 403/17.

European Parliament. (2016). *Financing of CSDP Missions and Operations.* European Parliamentary Research Service, PE577.958.

European People's Party. (2015, November). *Towards a European Defence Union.* Position Paper.

European Security Strategy. (2003, December 12). *A Secure Europe in a Better World: European Security Strategy.* Brussels, p. 1.

Fiott, D. (2017, April 2). The CARD on the EU Defence Table. *ISS Issue Alert,* No. 10. Paris: EU Institute for Security Studies.

Gentiloni, P. (2016, September 15). EU Needs 'Schengen for Defense'. *Politico.*

Joint Declaration. (2016, July 8). *Joint Declaration by the President of the European Council, the President of the European Commission, and the Secretary-General of the North Atlantic Treaty Organisation.* Press Release (2016) 119, Warsaw.

Juncker, J-C. (2016, September 14). *State of the Union Address 2016: Towards a Better Europe – A Europe That Protects, Empowers and Defends.* Strasbourg.

Marrone, A., & Camporini, V. (2016, November 19). *Recent Developments in Italy's Security and Defence Policy.* Rome: Istituto Affari Internazionali.

Mogherini. (2017, 23 November). *Remarks by the High-Representative/Vice-President Federica Mogherini at the 2017 Annual Conference of the European Defence Agency.* Brussels.

Strategic Review. (2015, July). *The European Union in a Changing Global Environment: A More Connected, Contested and Complex World.* European External Action Service.

UK Government. (2018, July). *The Future Relationship Between the United Kingdom and the European Union*. Cm 9593.

von der Leyen, U., & le Drian, J.-V. (2016, September 11). *Joint Position by Defence Ministers Ursula von der Leyen and Jean Yves le Drian, Revitalizing CSDP. Towards a Comprehensive, Realistic and Credible Defence in the EU*. Retrieved from https://www.senato.it/japp/bgt/showdoc/17/DOSSIER/990802/3_propositions-franco-allemandes-sur-la-defense.pdf.

CHAPTER 3

Brexit, Defence Expenditure and Defence Industries

The macroeconomic impact of Brexit upon the UK and the EU compared to the *status quo* is subject to contestation. For instance, Patrick Minford, Chair of Economists for Free Trade, argues that 'a "hard" Brexit is good for the UK economically while "soft" Brexit leaves us as badly-off as before' (Minford 2017, 3). By way of contrast George Osborne, as Chancellor of the Exchequer, concluded that 'none of the alternatives support trade and provide influence on the world stage in the same way as continued membership of a reformed EU' (UK Government 2016a, 5). The longer-term impact will depend upon the nature of any agreement (or the lack thereof) and the degree of access to the UK's access to the EU.

The case for the unique partnership sought by the UK government in security and defence with the EU will be complicated by serious questions about whether the UK can actually afford the ambitions laid down in its 2015 SDSR which were calculated upon the assumption of potential savings in defence of up to £20 billion. Although the defence budget has been shielded from some of the deeper cuts elsewhere in the public sector (like police services, border control, customs and immigration), the Ministry of Defence's (MoD) new equipment commitments under the review amounted to around £24 billion, but with only £6 billion to actually fund this expenditure. No new resources for the first three years of the review period (2015–2018) were foreseen, with core defence spending set to fall by around 4% in real terms in 2016–2017. As Malcolm Chalmers (2017) observed, the MoD has been obliged to fund cost overruns by

© The Author(s) 2019
S. Duke, *Will Brexit Damage our Security and Defence?*,
https://doi.org/10.1007/978-3-319-96107-1_3

cutbacks in activity levels across the armed forces, while being mindful of the 2015 Conservative Party Manifesto which pledges not to reduce the number of regular service personnel to below 82,000.

Testimony to the House of Commons by General Sir Richard Barrons, former commander of the UK Joint Forces Command, reflected this analysis when he summarised the discussions surrounding UK capabilities as follows:

> So you end up with the risk of a ridiculous, zero-sum discussion both within the service-the nonsense of culling marines to buy more sailors—and between the services, which is why you end up generally with a current navy structurally underfunded, air force that is holding together with a bunch of very good equipment but at the end of its engineering and support capacity, and an army that, broadly speaking, is 20 years out of date. (MacAskill 2017)

These and other warnings about the risks of hollowed-out forces and even whether the UK will be able to sustain its NATO 2 percent of GDP on defence pledge, had the overall effect of challenging the UK's assumption that its military and more general security prowess deserves some form of unique post-Brexit recognition by the EU. Contrary, however, to this rather gloomy analysis, a National Security Capabilities Review elicited no such concerns when it stated that 'The fundamentals of our defence strategy within SDSR 2015 remain sound, including the development of Joint Force 2025' (UK Government 2018a, 14).[1]

When looked at in comparative terms with the EU27, the simple fact that the UK spends significantly more than any other EU member, including France, in terms of defence expenditure is of relevance. Moreover, the UK also showed a significant increase from 2014 to 2015, while France and Germany remained static and Italy declined (European Defence Agency 2016). When defence expenditure is considered as a percentage of GDP only 4 EU Member States reach the 2% of GDP guideline agreed to by NATO in Wales in 2014; they are Estonia, Greece, Poland and the United Kingdom.[2] The average for the EU27 (minus Denmark who does

[1] This includes a maritime task group centred on the Queen Elizabeth II aircraft carrier; a land division with 3 brigades including a new Strike Force; an air group of combat, transport and surveillance aircraft and a Special Forces Task Group.
[2] Romania is likely to reach the goal in 2018, while Latvia and Lithuania have committed to reaching it as well.

not participate in the EDA) is 1.4% for 2015. On a per capita basis, the UK outspent (€747 for 2014 and €809 for 2015) France by far (€592 for 2014 and €589 for 2015). When it comes to the total number of military personnel, however, the UK lags in fourth (behind France, Germany and Italy), all of whom have more active military personnel, but with France and Britain being far ahead when it comes to the number of deployable military personnel (both with over 60,000). France and the UK have comparable numbers of civilian personnel, but both lag appreciably behind Germany who had has almost 30,000 more.

Whether the UK will continue to fulfil its 2% pledge from outside the EU will depend upon a number of factors. As a member of NATO, the UK is likely to attach political importance to maintaining its obligation since, as Mogherini observed, this is 'a NATO debate' but, significantly, she added that if the European countries 'want to spend more and better, the only way in which they can do that is through the European Union' (EEAS 2018). Since the UK has vocally urged others to meet the goal, it may feel even more pressure to sustain its commitment from outside the Union. A more nuanced response might note that if an economic downturn follows the UK's formal departure from the EU in March 2019, defence expenditure as a proportion of GDP could still be maintained due to the overall shrinkage of the UK economy (since the percentage measure is only a proportionate amount and not a measure of overall defence expenditure).

Another critical variable is the value of the pound. It is possible that a further slide in sterling will complicate the UK's defence commitments under the 2015 SDSR since the cost of dollar denominated equipment in particular (such as the F-35 Joint Strike Fighters, Trident ballistic missiles, Protector UAV's or Apache helicopters) could imply additional and unforeseen costs for the UK's defence budget.[3] There are signs that this is already happening. Mark Lyall Grant, the Prime Minister's former national security adviser, warned that the weakened pound has 'blown a hole of up to £700 million a year in spending plans since the referendum, as expensive military kit is purchased in the US' (Savage 2017). The UK is, however, less exposed to defence imports denominated in euros, such as the

---

[3] For example, the MoD estimated that the cost of the Trident successor programme to be £25 billion. By 2015 and the SDSR the cost had risen to £31 billion. One estimate puts the eventual cost as high as £167 billion (see *SIPRI Yearbook 2016: Armaments, Disarmament and International Security*, pp. 630–631).

A-400M transport aircraft, with around £18.6 billion of the defence equipment plan denominated in dollars while around £2.6 billion is denominated in euros (Black et al. 2017, 38). For UK defence industries a falling pound may boost exports, but any short-term gains risk being wiped out by the cost of raw materials and parts from overseas, and in the longer-term by the possible relocation of European and other defence industrial interests currently in the UK.

In terms of the defence expenditure *within* the armed forces, the UK spends appreciably more than any other EU member on operation and maintenance (€16.7 million in 2014 and €19.5 million in 2015, compared to France who spent €7.1 million in 2014 and €9.6 million in 2015). The UK's expenditure on operation and maintenance as a proportion of overall defence expenditure is not the highest in the EU (Sweden and Hungary spend more) but it is significantly above the EU27 average. When considering defence investment, the UK spends less than France, but far more than Germany, and only slightly above the EU average as a percentage of overall defence expenditure. Expenditure on defence equipment procurement is roughly comparable between France and the UK, but well above third placed Germany, but as a percentage of total defence expenditure both are just above the EU27 average of 13.3% in 2014. France and the UK are, literally, in league of their own when it comes to expenditure on research and development (R&D) and both spend well above the EU average of 4.5% in 2014 (with France at 9.1% and the UK at 7.8%). France and the UK are again comparable when it comes to collaborative defence equipment procurement, with Italy in a distant third, followed by Spain and Sweden (this pattern should be of little surprise given the defence industrial interests of these countries). But, as a percentage of overall defence expenditure, Spain, Luxembourg, Belgium and Italy firmly lead France and the UK.

A further important matrix is the deployability of armed personnel. France had the highest numbers of troops deployed (20,900 in 2013 and 8752 in 2014), while the UK had 10,200 in 2013 dropping to 2300 in 2014—with the latter figure below Italy and just above Poland and Sweden. The numbers deployed can, however, be influenced by the end or start of an operation and the costs of deployment will also reflect the locale of operation. The overall number of deployable land forces is similar for France and the UK (with the former at 63,350 and the latter at 69,800 in 2014).

By any statistical indicator, as in those from the EDA, the UK is therefore a major general defence player. It has also been a significant player in some less obvious, even surprising, ways. For instance, when it comes to conforming with the Commission's 2009 directive that requires Member States to publish defence tenders and contracts in the same manner that applies to other public procurement, the UK accounts for 7.9% of contract notices, which is slightly less than Poland, but 55% of all notices are accounted for by France and Germany together (European Commission 2009). But, the UK also published more voluntary *ex ante* (VEAT) notices than any other Member State (452 compared to 92 for France and 3 for Germany) (European Parliament 2015, 22).[4]

In spite of the Commission's lack of response to non-compliance with the directive (and a following one in 2014) the UK has been one of the most vigorous supporters of the application of free-market principles to defence procurement. Even so, as the Commission ruefully noted, '80% of defence procurement continues to be run on a purely national basis and the resultant lack of cooperation between the EU Member States in defence and security is estimated to cost annually between €25–100 billion' (European Commission 2016, Annex). Even with the passage of several years since the directives, frequent use is still made of offset requirements to bolster national defence industries and jobs. In spite of some joint programmes, such as that on unmanned aerial vehicles (UAVs), the sobering fact remains that 'no single European country on its own will be able to sustain the full range of capabilities or the underlying industrial base' (European Political and Strategy Centre 2015, 6).

The statistics also suggests that the sheer political and defence industrial clout of France and Germany makes any talk of a European Defence Union meaningless without their cooperation. France and Germany are indeed beginning to cooperate together on questions of security and defence at the diplomatic level, notably in the Normandy format, and there is growing congruence on a number of strategic challenges like terrorism and irregular migration. When it comes to operational cooperation, however, Germany is simply not able to field significant expeditionary

---

[4]VEAT notices are those that apply to contracts awarded without prior publication, or to a contract by negotiated procedure without prior publication of a contract notice. In the event that the administrative court has not received an appeal within 10 days, the contract awarded without prior notice is not subject to review (this represents around 30% of the UK contract notices, but this still compares well to Romania and Italy where 71% and 80% of notices respectively were the result of a contract award without prior publication).

forces, notably in the face of *Bundestag* reluctance, and it has not stepped up to the plate in terms of defence expenditure and operational readiness or sustainability. But underlying the general statistics there are important differences between France and Germany over strategic focus (with France being primarily concerned with the Sahel whereas Germany, until recently, has less interest and experience), the use of force, the procedures for the release of military force for operations (via the Parliament in Germany and the President in France), disagreements about the export of jointly-produced defence goods, alongside France's military overstretch and Germany's deficient military equipment (Koenig and Walter-Franke 2017, 8–9). It is also not clear whether other EU members, such as the Visegrad countries, are particularly keen on the prospect of a Franco-German tandem driving European security and defence integration.

THE UK'S DEFENCE EXPENDITURE AND DEFENCE INDUSTRIAL INTERESTS

The general debate about Brexit's potential impact on defence expenditure was reflected in official outlets and the quality press, but the equally important debate surrounding the impact of Brexit on defence industries and cooperation with the EU was more muted. The UK government's September 2017 Partnership Paper certainly does not rule out *a priori* contributions to EU military operations or civilian missions. There is, however, far less specificity to this aspect of potential cooperation between with the EU post Brexit than there is on the defence industrial aspects where the government has taken a strong line on the importance of the UK's defence industries to the EU's ability to tackle current and future threats, its global competitiveness and its ability to be autonomous and effective, all of which demand 'the UK at the EU's side' (UK Government 2018b, 66).

The UK is Europe's leading exporter of military equipment ahead of both France and Russia and, over a rolling ten-year period (2007–2016), the UK was the second largest defence exporter globally (Fig. 3.1). The overall value of UK defence exports in 2016 moved it up to fifth place in the global rankings (behind the US, Japan, China and Germany). UK defence industries have an annual turn-over of around £65 billion supporting around 900,000 jobs and have created almost 10,000 apprenticeships (Defence Contracts Online 2016).

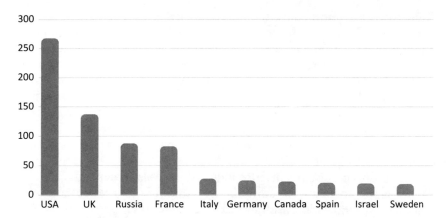

Fig. 3.1 Top ten defence exporters (based on orders/contracts signed 2007–2016) $billion. Source: UK Department for International Trade (2017), UK Defence and Security Export Statistics for 2016, released 25 July, p. 7

As with other facets of the Brexit debates, assessments of the likely defence-industrial impact differ. A worst-case analysis is tied to a 'no deal' scenario where the UK has to follow WTO rules, along with the possibility of deeper defence procurement integration within the EU excluding third parties like the UK (see Uttley and Wilkinson 2017, 491–502). More optimistically, one assessment envisages that EU-UK defence-industrial relations will not change that much and that the UK's withdrawal from the EU might even stimulate EU defence spending with possible positive spill-over effects for the UK (Calcara 2017, 139–152). The arguments presented below suggest a less rosy outcome due in large part to the potential exclusion of the UK from significant EU research and development funding with potentially negative effects for innovation and technology.

Europe is a relatively small defence export market for the UK, lagging significantly behind the Middle East (where Saudi Arabia, Qatar and the UAE are significant importers). The signature of a £5 billion deal in December 2017 with Qatar for 24 Typhoon fighters, Brimstone, Meteor missiles and Paveway IV bombs followed by the long-anticipated €6.9 billion memorandum of intent with Saudi Arabia in March 2018 for 48 Eurofighter Typhoon aircraft, underlines the importance of the region to UK defence exports. The Middle East represents 57% of UK defence exports for 2007–2016 and most of this comprises orders from Saudi Arabia. The Asia-Pacific region has also increased defence imports significantly (notably

South Korea) and now equals the European market for UK defence exports at around 10% for the same period. The North American market is notoriously difficult to penetrate and falls behind the UK's exports to Europe; but, the UK is still the largest European exporter to the North American market and it represents around 23% of UK defence exports in 2016. Of the top ten global defence importers for the decade, none are in Europe which suggests that the most valuable contracts will be found outside Europe in in Saudi Arabia, India, Qatar, North America, UAE, Iraq, Brazil and Egypt—all countries with high or increasing military expenditure (UK Department of International Trade 2017, 9).

The future of the UK's defence industrial sector will depend upon the nature of any Brexit and whether the UK continues to have access to the Single Market and if it successfully negotiates a free trade agreement (FTA) with the EU. The UK would be at a competitive disadvantage without a FTA since it may exclude Britain from any future large defence initiatives. The prospect of Brexit will certainly make it more difficult and unpredictable for European defence industries operating in the UK like Airbus, Thales, Leonardo-Finmeccanica or MDBA, as well as for British defence industries who are involved in collaborative projects.

Put, however, in terms of the wider UK economy, defence industries may not be as vulnerable compared to other sectors that are more exposed to trade with the EU. It may therefore be possible to reorient UK defence exports to the higher growth markets in the Middle East and North America. Europe has anyway proven a hard market to penetrate due to the unusually high levels of market protection that exist where national security grounds are frequently invoked to avoid open competition. But, the area where the UK is likely to lose out will be research and development, including access to EU research funding through the EU's Preparatory Action on Defence Research and Horizon 2020. With regard to the latter, however, it is possible that the UK could negotiate some form of associated status as Israel, Norway and Switzerland have done. But, this would mean contributing to the overall research budget based on GDP and, most probably, accepting freedom of movement, all without being able to establish research priorities. Alternatively, the UK could establish subsidiaries in EU Member States who would be eligible for research funding. The uncertainties surrounding the UK's access to research funding post-Brexit and its ability to contribute to the development of cutting-edge technologies may have knock-on effects for large joint-procurement programmes within the EU. An interesting case study in this regard is the aerospace sector.

The Critical Case of Aerospace

The UK's defence export performance is heavily dependent upon the aerospace sector, which in 2007–2016 accounted for 85% of all defence exports (whereas globally this sector represents around 63% of all defence sales) and it is worth around £14 billion annually (House of Commons 2017a). The export of land and sea defence products remains relatively minor (at 8% and 7% respectively for the period) (UK Department of International Trade 2017, 12). It is, however, clear that the UK has been trying to decrease its reliance on the aerospace sector (by 18% from 2015–2016) in an attempt to rebalance its portfolio. Even so, these are sectors that are traditionally long-cycle given the time involved in developing, testing and placing new products onto the defence markets. The aerospace and defence industry in the UK represents approximately 363,000 jobs, with a turnover of £72 billion (€94 billion), of which £37 billion (€48 billion) was exported (Deloitte 2017). The prospect of Brexit may have several implications for this particular sector. Three stand out.

First, defence industries are fiercely competitive and involve considerable amounts of investment to develop new capabilities and technologies. The prospect of EU-funded research and development, via the Commission's new European Development Fund, may give EU competitors an advantage when it comes to both the development but also the testing of new technologies. This has to be combined with a decline in UK 'high value design' in this sector, which has fallen by 30% between 1990–2015. This downward trend is 'primarily linked to the shrinking presence of OEMs within the UK and a reduction in UK-controlled aerospace capability due to past and on-going acquisitions by foreign competitors' (Berger 2017, 6). The UK also lags behind when it comes to engine and system test rigs, large scale demonstrators and production technology centres when compared to much of the European competition (Berger 2017, 13). This could imply that Airbus, with two large plants in the UK at Broughton and Filton, may face pressure to relocate to France, Germany or Spain as the possible result of post-Brexit non-tariff barriers. Although these are civilian plants, the overall economic impact of plant closures or relocation could have a knock-on impact on defence through the loss of transferable skills (such as wing-related technologies). Even in the space sector there are already Brexit-related ramifications, such as those for businesses working on the Galileo project who are now required to indicate where they will locate their supply chains post March 2019 in order to bid for work. There are uncertainties regarding continued access to Horizon 2020 funding which is significant for this sector. Brexit also implies that the back-up site for the Galileo Security Monitoring Centre will have to be relocated from the UK to Spain (the main site is in France).

Second, potential restrictions on the freedom of movement of employees post-Brexit may damage the competitiveness of companies like Rolls-Royce where approximately a quarter of the work force is in the EU (Hollinger 2017). In an industry that relies upon mobility to solve temporary production challenges, the ability to move key workers around may make the UK less attractive as a key component or engine manufacturing base. The UK aerospace industry is also reliant upon specialist overseas talent in key areas for development and research with around 4% of aerospace and defence employees coming from the EU (Deloitte 2017). This is a critical point when the UK suffers from well-publicised shortages in key technological areas (UK Government 2016b). Research funding through Horizon 2020 is worth around £100 million per annum to the UK aerospace industry (House of Commons 2017a). The prospect of more difficult access to research funding, non-UK talent and the prospect of non-tariff barriers caused, for instance, by long delays at borders if the UK is outside the Customs Union, will make the UK aerospace sector, including its defence sector, potentially less competitive.

Third, the prospect of Brexit also muddies the regulatory environment. For instance, it is uncertain whether the UK will continue its membership of the European Aviation Safety Agency (EASA) which will have an impact upon not only European partners but also beyond (for instance, the 170 repair locations in the UK licenced by the US Federal Aviation Administration are certified through EASA). Non-UK membership of EASA would make collaboration at the EU level difficult but need not exclude a bilateral agreement, like that with Switzerland, which would have to be negotiated well in advance of March 2019. Again, sticking with the aerospace sector, the Anglo-French Unmanned Combat Air Vehicle (UCAV) serves as an interesting test case. The Anglo-French partnership between Dassault and British Aerospace (BAE) Systems is part of the future combat air system (FCAS) initiative agreed to by the respective governments in 2014 and reaffirmed in March 2016 at a summit in Amiens (Perry 2017).[5] The future of the combat drone project is in doubt and even if it is argued that the FCAS falls outside the confines of Brexit, there are still profound uncertainties regarding the basis of collaboration and potential costs that might be involved. Continuation of the project could represent contracts for Safran and Rolls-Royce to develop engines for the prototypes. The project is currently in Phase 1 which commenced at the end of 2017 with the objective of having two demonstrators flying by 2025. The demonstration models will use a common airframe, but the radar, electronic warfare and optronic sensors, could differ and, on any advanced versions, they may differ in other ways to give national defence contractors a greater role based on national requirements (Osborne 2016). Failure of the project could leave France with a go-it-alone option, but with all of the associated costs. Alternatively, the UK could decide to simply go with American options. The latter may have some appeal, particularly given the relative success of the UK in penetrating the North America defence market.

The future of the unmanned FCAS has been cast into further doubt by the July 2017 Franco-German initiative to develop a manned successor to the Dassault Rafale and Eurofighter Typhoon which, confusingly, is also called FCAS. France and Germany have also agreed to cooperate on the next version of the Airbus Tiger attack helicopter, air-to-ground missiles, a medium-altitude long-endurance drone (with Italy and Spain) and joint acquisition of tanks and artillery. The initiative is in the early stages and major hurdles will need to be crossed, such as finding agreement on export regulations, which could complicate transatlantic relations with the US aggressively pushing the Lockheed Martin F-35 option to its NATO allies, with some interest from Germany and a commitment from the UK to purchase 138 F-35B's (the short take-off and vertical landing variant). More to the point, around 15% of all F-35 production will take place in the UK employing around 1800 people and more will be employed in the global repair hub for Europe-based F-35s (House of Commons 2017b, 35). If the Franco-German fighter jet is to become a reality, it will require collaboration between the Airbus Group and Dassault Aviation including an understanding on their respective roles. The Franco-German FCAS is designed to

[5] This should not be confused with the identically named 2016 Airbus FCAS concept to provide the Bundeswehr with a potential successor to the Tornado. In this case the FCAS would be a manned system.

not only meet the future demands of the two countries but also ensure that Europe retains control over its weapons systems. It also raises major questions for the UK's attractiveness as a potential post-Brexit partner and its ability to compete in the aerospace sector from outside the EU.

CONCLUSIONS

The economics of the UK's national security is likely to emerge as a more general point of concern as budgets are subject to increasing pressure and debates over strategic prioritisation. As Malcolm Chalmers observed, 'Brexit is also likely to add new demands for investment in security-related capabilities, for example in relation to border control, customs and immigration services' (Chalmers 2017, 5). Given that the Home Office budget fell by 25% in real terms between 2010–2011 and 2015–2016, any increases in this budget could create pressure to reallocate funding from other parts of the security and defence budgets. 'Leave' advocates will no doubt observe that the cessation of payments to the EU's budget, of around £10 billion, could usefully be used to support national security and other programmes. This is correct, but only if any nominal 'gains' will not be wiped out by the costs of the 'divorce bill' (i.e. the amount of money that the UK owes the EU for its commitments under the current EU multiannual financial framework which ends in 2020) or a more general post-Brexit economic recession in the UK.

The aerospace sector remains critical not only for UK exports, since it is not only the country's top manufacturing subsector, but also because of the technological skills involved. The stakes for the UK are high if it is no longer a member of EASA, since it is currently a major contributor to current safety standards and, if outside, it would have to re-apply for certification and will also fall outside the EU-US bilateral safety agreement. The UK defence sector may also be hurt by its inability to access vital research funding, notably the European Commission's EDF, which may leave some of the larger EU27 members at a competitive advantage. In the event of a messy Brexit, the EU may face tariff barriers for UK components or goods which will also slow production and increase costs, thus making the UK a less valuable partner for the larger European consortia. The UK also benefits from access to critical knowledge and skills from the EU which, in the event of restrictions on the free movement of people, will further damage UK competitiveness. For the larger UK defence industries, one of the options may be to consider relocating production facilities out of the UK if the right personnel cannot be found or attracted to the UK, or if the costs of manufacturing become disadvantageous. The possibility of further Franco-German cooperation on major weapons systems may also face the UK with the stark choice of developing systems alone, or in consortia that may include non-EU partners, or purchasing US systems. The possibility of the UK negotiating an administrative agreement with the EDA that would permit UK participation in PESCO and access to EDF should be explored, as was advocated in the previous chapter, but it should be noted that many of the 'big ticket' items discussed above lay beyond the existing scope of these initiatives.

The UK may be able to exploit its post-Brexit freedom from the common 2009 EU export criteria and controls on the transfer of military goods. The situation with regard to dual-use goods (those with both civilian and military applications) will be delicate since the common commercial policy falls under the exclusive competence of the Union, for the civilian aspects, while the military applications do not. This would therefore have to be carefully negotiated as part of any prospective EU-UK trade agreement. The UK may adopt a national regulation which, instead of drawing on the 2009 Council regulation, would be based on international export regimes. Initially, there are likely to be few issues since the strategic export control lists are aligned between the EU and the UK (Department for International Trade 2018). This will obviously change with Brexit, with implications for the regulation and licensing of these goods. End-user controls (certifying that a buyer is the final recipient of materials) will also have to be reviewed. Related to this is the issue of whether the UK will continue to associate with sanctions in force that apply to defence-related or dual-purpose goods and non-proliferation considerations. Some form of post-Brexit regulatory alignment is clearly desirable, as is the harmonisation of enforcement (which is carried out at the national level) in order to avoid the targeting of countries where controls are perceived to be weakest.

References

Berger, R. (2017). *High Value Design: A Strategic Capability in the Global Competition for the Next Generation of Aircraft.* Aerospace Technology Institute.

Black, J., Hall, A., Cox, K., Kepe, M., & Silversten, E. (2017). *Defence and Security After Brexit: Understanding the Possible Implications of the UK's Decision to Leave the EU.* Compendium Report, RAND Europe.

Calcara, A. (2017). Brexit: What Impact on Armaments Cooperation? *Global Affairs, 3*(2), 139–152.

Chalmers, M. (2017, May). *Still International by Design?* RUSI Briefing Paper.

Defence Contracts Online. (2016). *Brexit: The Impact on the Defence Industry.* Defence Contracts Online. Retrieved from https://www.contracts.mod.uk/do-features-and-articles/brexit-the-impact-on-the-defence-industry/.

Deloitte. (2017). *Impact of Brexit on the Manufacturing Industry: Aerospace and Defence.* Retrieved from https://www2.deloitte.com/content/dam/Deloitte/uk/Documents/manufacturing/deloitte-uk-brexit-ad-sheet.pdf.

Department for International Trade. (2018, March). *UK Strategic Export Controls Lists.* Retrieved from https://assets.publishing.service.gov.uk/government/uploads/system/uploads/attachment_data/file/685044/control-list20180305.pdf.

EEAS. (2018, February 18). *Speech by Federica Mogherini at the Munich Security Conference.* Munich.

European Commission. (2009, June 10). Directive 2009/43/EC of the European Parliament and of the Council of 6 May 2009 Simplifying Terms and Conditions of Transfers of Defence-Related Products Within the Community. *Official Journal of the EU* L 146.

European Commission. (2016). *European Defence Action Plan: Towards a European Defence Fund.* Brussels, Press Release, IP/16/4088.

European Defence Agency. (2016, June 20). *National Defence Data 2013–2014 and 2015 (est.).*

European Parliament. (2015, June). *The Impact of the 'Defence Package' Directives on European Defence.* Directorate-General for External Policies, PE549.044.

European Political and Strategy Centre. (2015, June 15). In Defence of Europe: Defence Integration as a Response to Europe's Strategic Moment. *EPSC Strategic Notes,* Issue 4, European Political Strategy Centre.

Hollinger, P. (2017, January 4). UK Aerospace Industry Fears Loss of Leading Edge After Brexit. *Financial Times.*

House of Commons. (2017a, November 21). *Oral Evidence: Leaving the EU Implications for the Aerospace Industry, Business, Energy and Industrial Strategy Committee.* HC 380.

House of Commons. (2017b, December 19). *Unclear for Take-off? F-35 Procurement.* Defence Committee, Second Report of Session 2017–19, HC 326.

Koenig, N., & Walter-Franke, M. (2017, July 19). *France and Germany: Spearheading a European Security and Defence Union?* Policy Paper 202, Berlin: Jacques Delors Institute.

MacAskill, E. (2017, November 14). British Forces no Longer Fit for Purpose, Fomer UK Service Chiefs Warn. *The Guardian.*

Minford, P. (2017, August). *From Project Fear to Project Prosperity: An Introduction.* Retrieved from https://www.economistsforfreetrade.com/wp-content/

uploads/2017/08/From-Project-Fear-to-Project-Prosperity-An-Introduction-15-Aug-17-2.pdf.

Osborne, T. (2016, June 20). Engine, Planform Begin Shaping Anglo-French UCAV. *Aviation Week Network.* Retrieved from http://aviationweek.com/paris-air-show-2017/engine-planform-begin-shaping-anglo-french-ucav.

Perry, D. (2017, March 10). Dassault Plays Down Brexit Fears over Anglo-French UCAV Project. *Flight Global.* Retrieved from https://www.flightglobal.com/news/articles/dassault-plays-down-brexit-fears-over-anglo-french-u-435036/.

Savage, M. (2017, October 14). PM's Former Security Adviser Warns of Brexit Defence Cuts. *The Guardian.*

UK Department of International Trade. (2017, July 25). *UK Defence and Security Export Statistics for 2016.* Retrieved from https://www.gov.uk/government/uploads/system/uploads/attachment_data/file/631343/UK_defence_and_security_export_statistics_2016_Final_Version.pdf.

UK Government. (2016a, April). *HM Treasury Analysis: The Long-Term Economic Impact of EU Membership and the Alternatives.* CM 9250.

UK Government. (2016b). *Immigration Rules Appendix K: Shortage Occupation List.* Retrieved from https://www.gov.uk/guidance/immigration-rules/immigration-rules-appendix-k-shortage-occupation-list.

UK Government. (2018a, March). *National Security Capability Review.*

UK Government. (2018b, July). *The Future Relationship Between the United Kingdom and the European Union.* Cm 9593.

Uttley, M. R. H., & Wilkinson, B. (2017). Contingent Choices: The Future of United Kingdom Defence Procurement and Defence Industries in the Post-Brexit Era. *Global Affairs, 2*(5), 491–502.

CHAPTER 4

National Security and Brexit

The UK's proposals for post-Brexit engagement with the EU go beyond the external dimensions of security and defence to include a broader set of challenges such as cyber security, external migration, hybrid warfare, extremism and terrorism. These are often issues that typically preoccupy national security which, for any EU member, is the 'sole responsibility of each Member State' (Treaty on European Union Article 4.2). That said, it is also incumbent upon the EU to 'endeavour to ensure a high level of security through measures to prevent and combat crime … and through measures for coordination and cooperation between police and judicial authorities and other competent authorities…' (TFEU Article 67). This is broadly what the EU has tried to do without impinging upon national sovereignty.

Given the EU's competences in this area, alongside the UK's 'opt outs', the prospect of withdrawal from the EU could be expected to have relatively little impact on the UK's national security. By the same token it could be argued that Brexit will have a relatively minor effect on the internal security of the Union. This would, however, be wrong in both cases. On the UK side, there is strong interest on the part of security professionals to secure continued access to key EU organised crime, cybersecurity and counter-terrorism databases, alongside existing practical cooperation. As in external security, the May government is seeking 'a partnership that goes beyond any existing, often ad hoc arrangements for third-country relationships in this area' (UK Government 2017a, 2). The suggestion

© The Author(s) 2019
S. Duke, *Will Brexit Damage our Security and Defence?*,
https://doi.org/10.1007/978-3-319-96107-1_4

follows that such cooperation could be based on the 'legal models that the EU has used to structure cooperation with third countries in other fields, such as trade' (UK Government 2017a, 2). Although the government's partnership paper is vague on what type of trade-like agreement it has in mind, such agreements are anything but *ad hoc*, are often highly complicated, technical and take years to negotiate.

The impact of Brexit on national security has divided opinion, as Joanna Dawson observed:

> …proponents of Brexit have suggested that the UK's withdrawal from the EU will bring positive gains in the area of national security, allowing greater control over immigration and borders, and freedom from the jurisdiction of the Court with respect to issues such as data protection.
>
> Conversely, representatives from law enforcement and the security and intelligence communities have emphasised the importance of EU wide cooperation in tackling security threats, through the sharing of information and data, participation in agencies, and a coordinated strategy. The importance of British leadership and influence in this area has been repeatedly emphasised in evidence to parliamentary committees, and concerns expressed about the impact of its loss. (Dawson 2017, 3)

On the EU side, as the Council concluded in May 2017, the main interest is to enhance 'the EU's ability to act as a security provider, as well as its global strategic role and its capacity to act autonomously when and where necessary and with partners wherever possible' (Council of the EU 2017, 2). The areas in which the Council envisages improving cooperation with partner countries include, 'countering hybrid threats, strategic communications, cyber security, maritime security, security sector reform, border security, the external dimensions of irregular migration/human trafficking, the fight against organised crime and arms trafficking and preventing and countering radicalisation and terrorism' (Council of the EU 2017, 5). Within the potentially broad remit for cooperation one of the most urgent issues is to resolve the ambiguities surrounding specific borders.

BORDER ISSUES

The debate on both sides of the Brexit campaign leading to the referendum has often featured immigration and borders, often with little attempt to distinguish between legal and irregular migration, asylum seekers and refugees. In spite of the purported importance of the notion of taking back control of its borders, the UK's Border Force budget has been cut since 2012 from £617 million to £558 million in 2015–2016 (this covers most of the period when Theresa May was Home Secretary), which led to cuts to maritime and aerial surveillance (House of Commons 2016). This not only has implications for counter-terrorism and organised crime but may also have knock-on effects when the UK withdraws from the EU since extra personnel and resources are likely to be required for border and immigration procedures since substantial numbers will continue to cross to and from the EU's border each year when the UK has left the Union. This also makes the importance of establishing cross-border operational cooperation and data exchange between the EU and post-Brexit UK all the more pressing.

The associated debates on borders occasionally feature Calais, Cyprus and Gibraltar, but the issue of the future of the Common Travel Area and border arrangements between the Republic of Ireland and Northern Ireland has been the main preoccupation. At its most basic the border issue with Northern Ireland is that, post Brexit, Ireland and the UK may have a different legal status in the EU. Barring an agreement to the contrary, the 500-kilometre Derry to Dundalk border will become one of two external land borders of the EU and the UK (the other being Gibraltar).

The Brexit vote in Northern Ireland was 56% in favour of remain, with 44% favouring leave. Importantly, most of the Remain votes came from the nationalist and Catholic communities, while the Unionist communities were more divided, but still overall favoured leaving the EU. The devolved Northern Ireland Assembly had no influence over the government's decision to notify the UK's intention to withdraw from the EU under Article 50 of the Lisbon Treaty, although in theory it has influence in relation to the issue of whether Northern Ireland should remain part of the UK or become part of a united Ireland under the Good Friday Agreement, or Belfast Agreement, of 10 April 1998. In practice, the absence of a devolved assembly since its collapse over a year ago has led to *de facto* direct rule from Westminster. The particular status of the UK-Ireland relations are also addressed in Protocols 15 and 20 of the Lisbon Treaty.

The working assumption by the UK is that the Common Travel Area (CTA) between Ireland and Northern Ireland will continue beyond Brexit following assurances from the UK to this end (this is recognised in Article 2 of Protocol 20 of the Lisbon Treaty). The CTA, which was established in 1923, allows for roughly 30,000 to work and live on different sides of the border (European Parliament 2017). To put this into a broader perspective, there are around 110 million border-crossing every year (UK Government 2017b, 1). It is also worth recalling that, uniquely in the EU, almost 20% of Northern Ireland citizens are citizens of another EU state.

In the event of a 'no deal' scenario, it is difficult to envisage anything but the recreation of a real, as opposed to virtual, border since customs controls will be required, with entry and exit controls, between those within the Customs Union and those outside it. The government's position paper is unspecific about what security arrangements, like CCTV monitoring, should prevail post Brexit. But, in the absence of agreed solutions, the UK is committed to maintain 'fully alignment with those rules of the internal market and Customs Union which, now or in the future, support North-South cooperation, the all-island economy, and the protection of the Good Friday (Belfast) agreement' (European Commission 2017b, 9).

Within the UK the border issue is highly sensitive since the Conservative government of Theresa May is propped up by ten pro-Brexit Democratic Unionist Party (DUP) members who insist that Northern Ireland should leave the EU on the same terms as the rest of the UK. The outline of an agreement between the UK and the European Commission on the border issue of 8 December 2017 shows numerous holes and contradictions, most notably the UK is committed to protect the operation and institutions of the Good Friday agreement and to avoiding a 'hard border', which includes physical infrastructure, checks and controls. But, as the European Commission notes, 'This intention seems hard to reconcile with the United Kingdom's communicated decision to leave the internal market and Customs Union' (European Commission 2017b, 9). It is similarly difficult to understand that 'the commitments and principles in relation to Ireland/North Ireland will not pre-determine the outcome of wider discussions on the future EU-UK relationship' since Northern Ireland is an integral part of the UK (European Commission 2017b, 8). The possibility of a potential special deal for Northern Ireland was quickly noted by London and Scotland, who also saw majorities vote in favour of remain.

In security terms much will depend upon the actual type of border that emerges. The UK and the European Commission refer to the Good Friday agreement as a legal agreement, which it is, but it still takes political consensus to implement it. Anything that undermines the 'east-west' (Strand Three) dimensions of relations between Northern Ireland and Britain or the 'north-south' (Strand Two) aspects between the Republic of Ireland

and Northern Ireland, may threaten the stability of the power-sharing Assembly and Executive (Strand One) and, therefore, the agreement. In the absence of agreed solutions at the EU level the UK is 'committed to maintaining full alignment with those rules of the internal market and the Customs Union which, now or in the future, support North-South cooperation, the all-island economy and the protection of the Good Friday (Belfast) Agreement' (European Commission 2017b, 9). It is the unenviable task of Whitehall to balance the Commission's desire to protect Strand two along with the other strands.

If avoidance of the hard border and the continuation of something like the current border arrangements between Ireland and Northern Ireland is the shared goal between the EU and the UK, it suggests that *only* a soft Brexit is compatible with attaining this goal, in spite of the May government's protestations otherwise. In the event that this is not the case, the harder the border the more resistance can be expected. This could range from civil disobedience, as Sinn Féin has warned, growing black-market activities of the type that typified the pre-EEC border, disputes over the location of maritime borders and meridian lines, to renewed political and even nationalist tensions. Although the European Commission has made the case for continued PEACE IV funding, its discontinuation could put in danger those groups most vulnerable to the conflict legacy. There is an urgent need for some form of post-Brexit access to the European Arrest Warrant (EAW) which is a primary tool in the fight against terrorism and organised crime, including for police cooperation between Northern Ireland and the Republic. The EAW, established in 2002, provides for the extradition of alleged criminals from one EU member to another, but this critically depends upon the legal oversight of the European Court of Justice. Although extraditions can take place outside the EAW, they are more costly and time consuming.

A second security and border-related problem lies with Gibraltar which is a British Overseas territory. A number of Conservative politicians, including the Prime Minister, Michael Howard, the former Conservative Leader and Michael Fallon, the former UK's Defence Secretary, have made numerous pledges to protect the sovereignty of Gibraltar which voted 96% for Remain (Asthana 2017). Gibraltar is of considerable importance for UK security and defence since it hosts a Permanent Joint Operating Base contributing to the security and defence of the UK itself, as well as being strategically located at the entrance to both the Atlantic and the Mediterranean. The base includes runway facilities, signals posts, thirty miles of underground tunnels and a secure harbour which has played an important role in NATO operations, such as during the 2011 intervention in Libya where is supported British units and resupply services for U.S. navy submarines. A special "Z" birth is also available for carrying out repairs to British and American (non-nuclear) submarines (Black 2017). In spite of Spanish demands for some form of joint sovereignty over Gibraltar this remains unlikely since, in spite of the importance of cross-border trade, Gibraltar's economy 'remains dependent upon institutional separation from Spain ... so as to attract insurance and on-line gambling businesses' (Black et al. 2017, 115). Spain's adjoining region, Campo de Gibraltar, suffers from high unemployment which, in the event of the disruption of cross-border commerce and the daily passage of around 13,000 who cross the border to work in Gibraltar, would hurt both economies.

A third important border issue concerns Calais. The 2003 Treaty of Le Touquet between France and the UK permits mutual frontier controls in the territory of the other's seaports (this covers the functioning of the Eurotunnel, Eurostar as well as ferry services). The security concerns arise with the attempts by almost 13,000 to clandestinely enter the UK by either train or ferry in July 2015 alone (Migration Watch 2016). Since this is a bilateral treaty there should be no immediate effect due to the UK leaving the EU. Ironically, the existence of the 'Jungle' until 2016, as the camp just outside Calais ferry terminals was known, illustrated that it was far easier to enter illegally into the Schengen area that it was to Britain which has an 'opt out' and is therefore outside the area.[1] Brexit will not therefore change the underlying picture since the French port areas, as well as the entrance to the Channel tunnels, will remain an external border of the Schengen area but it may well cost the UK more. During a visit by President Macron to the UK in January 2018 France requested extra post-Brexit funding from the UK (around £45 million per annum) to defray the costs of extra security measures around the French port cities and has suggested the creation of a joint operational task force for processing asylum seekers in Calais. Beyond Calais, the UK will have to negotiate with France, Belgium and the Netherlands to safeguard services through the Channel Tunnel and with Ireland for the Belfast-Dublin Enterprise rail line.

Finally, the UK faces its own Brexit-related dispute with the Republic of Cyprus due to the sovereign base areas (SBAs) of Akrotiri and Dhekalia

---

[1] The camp was dismantled in 2016 but around 1000 refugees returned by the end of 2017.

in Cyprus, along with the corridor connecting the latter to Ayios Nikolaos. This issue concerns the 15,000 or so EU and Cypriot citizens living in or traversing into the SBAs although, from the European Commission's perspective, the protocol agreed to by Cyprus upon its accession to the EU should remain in force (European Commission 2018a, 107). It remains to be seen how this will affect UK-Cyprus relations and whether the UK is willing to negotiate on the partial surrender of residential parts of the bases that are no longer required for military operations (as was proposed in the earlier UN-backed Annan Plan). For its part, Cyprus remains concerned that concessions to the UK on security and defence may open the door for similar demands from Turkey.

SHARING INTELLIGENCE AND INFORMATION

By its own assessment the UK has been one of 'the leading contributors to the development, at an EU level, of practical, effective measures to strengthen information-sharing and cooperation' (UK Government 2017a, 4). For instance, on counter-terrorism and countering violent extremism the UK has worked closely with the EU and its CT coordinator. It has also contributed to the efforts of other countries to strengthen their CT capabilities and to adopt common approaches, often based on the UK's CT strategy (CONTEST). The UK participates in the EAW which facilitates the extradition of individuals between EU Member States to face prosecution or to serve a prison sentence for an existing eviction. In the period 2004–2016 this enabled the UK to extradite 7000 individuals accused or convicted of criminal offences in other EU countries (with 1000 coming from the EU to the UK to face justice) (House of Lords 2016a, 16). Police cooperation between Northern Ireland and Ireland under the EAW is an integral part of the political settlement. The UK has also been the most vigorous exponent in proposing autonomous EU sanctions as a foreign policy tool and that many of the asset freezes applied to terrorist organisations in the EU 'are based on UK national proscriptions' (UK Government 2017c, 7–8). But, post-Brexit participation in the EAW is incompatible with the UK government's determination to end the jurisdiction of the European Court of Justice.

The updated Schengen Information System (SIS II) is a further tool that supports external border control and law enforcement cooperation which has 22 EU participants, as well as four associated countries.[2] SIS II

[2] Iceland, Liechtenstein, Norway and Switzerland.

permits police or border authorities to enter or consult alerts on 35,000 wanted or missing persons, individuals subject to a EAW as well as objects (like vehicles or firearms). It was consulted 2.9 billion times in 2015. The UK connected to SIS II in April 2015 and over 6400 foreign alerts received hits in the UK over the following year, and over 6600 UK-issued alerts received hits in other EU members (House of Lords 2016a, 17). SIS II is also of value to the UK since it includes a facility to issue discreet alerts to police and border forces in relation to counter-terrorism suspects. When it comes to criminal records the UK, along with other EU members, has access to the European Criminal Records Information System (ECRIS), which is a decentralised information system open to nearly all EU members, providing judges and magistrates with criminal records of persons, regardless of which state the crime was committed in. The UK is one of the most active members of ECRIS and the government has therefore proposed continued participation as part of a new legal relationship.

Similarly, the UK has played a significant role in the EU's efforts to tackle serious and organised crime, including delivering the EU's Policy Cycle for Serious and Organised Crime. The UK is a member of the EU Agency for Law Enforcement and Cooperation (Europol), an EU agency that assists Member States' law enforcement agencies in addressing cross-border crime with the aim of preventing serious and organised crime and terrorism. All members have access to the Europol Information Service (EIS) which is a central criminal intelligence database covering all areas of the agency's remit. The UK is again one of the largest contributors of data, information and expertise.

When it comes to cyber security the UK has contributed expertise and experience to develop the EU's Network and Information Security (NIS) Directive and participates in developing NIS Computer Security and Incident Response Teams (CSIRT). The UK is a 'major contributor' to the EU Agency for Network and Information Security (ENISA) (UK Government 2017c, 13). The UK was also instrumental in establishing the Joint Cybercrime Action Task Force and the Europol Internet Referral Unit in 2014 and 2015 respectively. Any continued access, or contributions, to cybersecurity will again depend upon a negotiated agreement between the UK and the EU with the obvious proviso that any such agreement is likely to be based on compliance with EU data protection and privacy standards.

Europol has, on average, carried out 18,000 cross-border investigations per annum in response to terrorist, drug trafficking, money laundering, organised fraud, counterfeiting and people smuggling activities. In addition, it is worth briefly mentioning Europol's database of foreign fighters and suspected terrorists. The UK is one of the heaviest, if not the heaviest, user of Europol facilities and support (House of Lords 2016b, 17). The UK joined the updated Europol framework in May 2017 since the UK's collaboration with Europol would otherwise have ended. Brandon Lewis, the UK's Policing minister explained that the UK may be leaving the EU but 'the reality of cross-border crime remains' and that 'Europol provides a valuable service to the UK' (Warrell 2017). The UK wishes to negotiate a 'bespoke' agreement with Europol although, as Michel Barnier (2017) has made abundantly clear, full membership is not open to non-EU members (2017). The European Commission's draft withdrawal agreement is equally firm that at the end of the transition period (31 December 2020) the UK shall 'cease to be entitled to access any network, any information system, and any database established on the basis of Union law' (European Commission 2018a, Article 7).

The details of any 'bespoke' agreement have obviously to be determined, but the Danish case has surfaced as a potential model for post-Brexit UK cooperation with Europol. Following a referendum in December 2015 Danish voters decided to retain an opt-out on EU cooperation on Justice and Home Affairs issues. In practical terms this implied that Denmark would normally leave Europol on 1 May 2017 when the Agency's new rules entered into force. Under a joint declaration between the EU and the Danish government signed in December 2016, Denmark formally left Europol in May 2017 but gained the right as a 'third-state' to exchange information, but will not have direct access to the Europol database. Instead Denmark can contact Danish-speaking Europol staff on a case-by-case basis to check the database and to add items on behalf of the Danish police and has observer status at the agency's Management Board and working groups. The applicability of this case to that of the UK once it leaves the EU is open to doubt, especially since the EU-Danish agreement depends upon Denmark's continued membership of the Schengen area, the implementation of the EU's directive on data protection into Danish law and acceptance of the jurisdiction of the ECJ—conditions that either inapplicable, or likely to be unworkable, in a post-Brexit context unless some form of joint jurisdiction can be agreed upon (House of Commons 2017, 83–89).

Not all, however, agree about the overall value of information exchanged at the European level. For instance, Sir Richard Dearlove, a former MI6 head, argued that there may in fact be national security benefits to Brexit, especially from the ability to dump the European Convention on Human Rights and the enhanced control that Brexit would afford over immigration (Dearlove 2016). In a further sign of how split the establishment is a successor in his post, John Sawers, concluded that, 'it would be odd for a British patriot to want to unwind what we now have. The costs would be clear and high. The alleged benefits would be uncertain' (Sawers 2016). Among the EU27 the UK's 'restrictive approach towards data-sharing on counter-terrorism through EU mechanisms' has also attracted criticism. More generally, the UK has developed a reputation as something of a database 'free-rider' based upon what some see as its meagre contributions; something that the UK has tried to amend in recent years (Dassù et al. 2018, 5).

Many of the UK's contributions to the databases named above involve the exchange of intelligence, complemented on the external security and defence side by the exchange of the analysis and intelligence with specialist bodies in the EEAS and European Commission. The UK's external intelligence links are, however, often portrayed through its extensive links with the US, rather than its European counterparts. In particular the 'Five Eyes' agreement, made in 1946 between Australia, Canada, New Zealand, the UK and the US to exchange various forms of intelligence, features (see Duke 2014, 242–260). This often throws up a somewhat distorted either-or equation, when in fact the situation is subtler, as the European Parliament indicated:

> There would be no reason for the United Kingdom to forfeit information of interest to its intelligence services, and, since that information would always remain secret, espionage under the UKUSA Agreement would not rule out an official policy of loyalty vis-à-vis Europe. (European Parliament 2001, 68)

But, the same report adroitly noted that, 'Closer EU cooperation in the field of intelligence may therefore constitute a serious test of the European ambitions of the United Kingdom and of the EU's capacity for integration' (European Parliament 2001, 131). As valuable as the extensive intelligence links between the UK and the US are, they have thrown up occasionally awkward questions. In the case of the US National Security Agency (NSA) the Echelon affair, which concerned the systematic interception of large amounts of private and commercial information by the

NSA, with the support of a UK facilities at Menwith Hill and Morwenstow, led to doubts about the trustworthiness of the UK. In a major report on the affair the European Parliament concluded that 'the existence of a global system for intercepting communications' operating with the participation of the 'Five Eyes' countries, is not in doubt (European Parliament 2001, 15). In this context the UK Government Communication Headquarters (GCHQ) 'Tempora' internet surveillance programme, involving the direct interception and sharing with the NSA of fibre optic cable bulk traffic, also came under negative scrutiny and censure in 2015 (Eden 2015). With regard to the Central Intelligence Agency (CIA), the frequent use of UK airports over the period of a decade for 'rendition' flights which were associated with the kidnapping and unlawful transfer of detainees, including to countries where they faced torture, also led to criticism. Over 50 airports and around 84 aircraft were allegedly used for renditions in the aftermath of the September 11 attacks, with Luton, Prestwick and Stanstead being the most used (Cobain and Ball 2013).

The overarching attention paid to UK-US intelligence ties tends to distract attention from the advances in intelligence analysis and sharing at the European level. In addition to Europol's intelligence role, noted above, the EU Intelligence Analysis Centre (INTCEN), the Intelligence Division of the EU Military Staff (EUMS) and the EU Satellite Centre (EUSC) all play an active role in the handling of sensitive information, including the analysis of intelligence. None of them is involved in the generation of raw intelligence which, rightly, belongs to the national level. But, all are involved in the production of analytic intelligence deriving from one or more sources. The civilian and military streams of intelligence analysis led to the establishment of a Single Intelligence Analysis Capacity (SIAC) in 2007 with the 'aim of optimizing the information available from both sources and distributing the best possible analysis to the various EU clients through joint intelligence products' (Duke 2014, 254).

The strength of the EU's growing ability to produce synthetic intelligence products based on multiple national intelligence products, lies in the ability to 'cross-check and validate intelligence analysis deriving from national sources' where purely national efforts may imply that 'individual agencies miss critical parts of the wider jigsaw puzzle' (Duke 2014, 257). The emphasis upon cross-border challenges to national security also suggests that the sharing of data via the EAW, ECRIS, PNR, SIS II and Europol has a particularly valuable role to play for the EU and the UK alike. This point was underlined emphatically by the respective heads of the intelligence services of France, Germany and the UK in an extraordinary press statement which argued that, 'Even after the UK's exit from the EU, close cooperation and cross-border information sharing must be taken forward on themes such as international terrorism, illegal migration, proliferation and cyber attacks' (Bundesnachrichtendienst 2018). A level of intelligence cooperation may therefore be foreseen, but not at the expense of the ability of the EU to autonomously assess its internal and external security environment (European Commission 2018b).

In addition to the above cooperation, the 2008 Prüm Decisions facilitate reciprocal searches of databases on DNA profiles, fingerprints and vehicle registration data for the investigation of crimes. It was the UK Home Secretary, Theresa May, who welcomed the UK's re-joining Prüm in 2015 when she observed that 'it will be quicker and easier for our police to check the national databases of other member states, hugely increasing the reach of UK law enforcement' (House of Lords 2015). The same effect could possibly be attained post-Brexit but only by negotiating individual agreements with all of the governments involved. In those cases where evidence of crime involving a foreign national in the UK is detected, separate extradition arrangements may also have to be negotiated. Similar observations apply to the European Dactyloscopy (Eurodac), a mechanism for sharing fingerprint data for asylum and law-enforcement purposes.

Quite aside from any intelligence benefits that the various databases offer UK national security, the UK has also enjoyed considerable influence in the EU's Justice and Home Affairs area including, until recently, through the Welsh director of Europol, Rob Wainwright. The same cannot be said of Julian King, Commissioner for Security who, given the circumstances, is 'not an effective champion for closer cooperation among EU member countries' (Paravicini 2017). King's experience as the UK's last Commissioner is a reminder that the UK will not exert anything like the same influence from outside the EU and, depending upon the nature and tone of any ongoing Brexit negotiations, the ability of the UK to simultaneously negotiate access to the various databases outlined above, as well as to contribute to them, may be compromised. The UK's July 2018 White Paper proposes developing mechanisms for rapid and secure data exchange, measures to support cross-border cooperation and continued cooperation with EU law enforcement and criminal justice agencies (UK Government 2018b, 55). But the details of how to do this remain vague, as do any necessary legal arrangements. On the EU side, post-Brexit relations may also be complicated by the need to respect the separate legal systems in Northern Ireland and Scotland (including the role of the Lord Advocate in the case of the latter). It should also be noted that Security of Information Agreement, facilitating the exchange of information between London and the EEAS, will cease with Brexit as will the UK's connection to the *Correspondance Europeenne* telex network for diplomatic traffic between London and most of the EU's institutions. There is therefore the urgent need for a new Security of Information Agreement on the exchange and protection of classified information, as has been advocated in London and Brussels.

The process for securing the agreements is also uncertain since, from 1 May 2017, Europol, for example, was not in a position to conclude direct agreements with third countries and they must now be negotiated as international agreements with the EU. This will imply that the necessary data protection standards and safeguards, based on a new EU regulation and directive which were both agreed to in 2016 and entered into force in May 2018, will be subject to an adequacy decision by the EU with the UK as a third country, or individual data controllers and processors will have to establish safeguards demonstrating that they provide adequate protection for date transferred outside the EU.[3] There are examples of third parties, like the U.S. negotiating access to some EU databases (as in the Privacy Shield or the Umbrella Agreement) but both took years to negotiate, with the latter taking five years—well beyond the two-year timeframe stipulated by the Lisbon Treaty's Article 50 for the UK's withdrawal from the EU. With regard to the Privacy Shield, an earlier version called 'Safe Harbour', contains a cautionary note. In *Schrems v Data Protection Commissioner*, the ECJ invalidated 'Safe Harbour', since the scheme 'thus enables interference, by United States public authorities, with the fundamental rights of persons, and the Commission decision does not refer either to the existence, in the United States, of rules intended to limit any such interference or to the existence of effective legal protection against the interference' (Court of Justice of the EU 2015). A more recent case, involving Canada, raised concerns over its full compatibility with EU data protection provisions, offering a further salutary cautionary note (Court of Justice of the EU 2016). Both cases strongly suggest that the UK's

---

[3] An adequacy decision refers in particular to Article 45 of the General Data Protection Regulation and Article 36 of the Police and Criminal Justice Directive, but these can only be negotiated once the UK is a non-member.

post-Brexit third party status will not make it immune to compliance with the ECJ or rulings by the Court and make the negotiation of any 'bespoke' agreement challenging.

CONCLUSIONS

It is clear that the UK has a strong interest in continued access to the specialised databases mentioned above, as well as to contribute information to them. In a post-Brexit scenario, the UK will therefore have to negotiate cooperation agreements with Europol including some form of access to the European Arrest Warrant, the SIS II database, and various other information systems that are of value to the UK and its national interests. This will pose challenges to the UK as a non-EU and non-Schengen member but it by no means unthinkable since Norway, Switzerland and the US have agreements that allow for limited forms of cooperation. Continued access to SIS II and ECRIS, which are of most importance to the UK, would require a unique agreement since there are no examples of access by non-Schengen or non-EU countries in either case.

An agreement on PNR might be slightly simpler, as in the cases of the EU agreements with Australia and the US, but the question of whether the UK should have access to intra-EU data may well surface and the disputes surrounding the EU-Canada PNR agreement do not bode well. Continued association with the Prüm decisions may be possible along the lines negotiated with Iceland and Norway since, unlike SIS II, there is no direct link to the Schengen *acquis* (see House of Lords 2016b). Similarly, cooperation on mutual legal assistance, following the precedents like Iceland, Japan or Norway, is also quite possible. Although existing agreements could provide potential models, they do not provide the unique agreement that the UK government has demanded.

Whether agreements can be found will ultimately depend upon the interest in continuing EU access to UK expertise and data, which are considerable, and this is likely to require a bespoke arrangement. Two major obstacles to any such cooperation have been identified. First, the EU will wish to be reassured that any EU information transferred to the UK will meet adequate data protection and privacy standards as determined by the European Commission. Since it is hard in practice to distinguish security-related data, any agreement will extend to commercial data. This does not exclude completely the idea of some form of bespoke regulatory alignment arrangement between the EU and the UK, but the European Commission is likely to be predictably wary of creating a potential pathway for other third-parties, thus potentially weakening the ECJ's oversight function.

Second, and related to the previous point, the UK's Data Protection Bill is likely to demonstrate automatic alignment with the EU framework, but the EU is still likely to demand proof of the UK's willingness to recognize the rulings of the ECJ if it wishes to maintain equivalent levels of cooperation on counter-terrorism, organised crime and access to the relevant databases post-Brexit. It may also lead to renewed concerns about mass surveillance by the UK government. Prime Minister May has promised to be 'respectful of the sovereignty of both the UK and the EU's legal orders' and that the UK will 'respect the remit of the European Court of Justice' when participating in EU agencies (UK Government 2018a). But, it remains to be seen how this will sit with hard-line Brexiteers, especially since 'control of its own laws' and 'ending the jurisdiction of the European Court of Justice in Britain' was one of the main guiding principles underpinning Brexit (UK Government 2017d). Indeed, the government's own future partnership paper in this area also notes that, 'When the UK leaves the EU, the legal framework that currently underpins cooperation between the UK and the EU on security, law enforcement and criminal justice will no longer apply to the UK' (UK Government 2017a).

The process can begin in earnest once the UK formally leaves the EU, but it is one that may well prove demanding and there are few non-EU/ Schengen cases that have satisfied the Commission's adequacy requirements (European Commission 2017a).[4] Given that over three-quarters of the UK's data flows are with EU countries, it is difficult to see how the post-Brexit UK could maintain such exchanges without an adequacy agreement. In its absence, it will be difficult for the UK to maintain, deepen and strengthen operation and practical cooperation and the UK and the EU risk becoming more attractive to terrorists and organised crime.

[4] They include Andorra, Argentina, Canada (partial), the Faroe Islands, Guernsey, Israel, the Isle of Man and New Zealand, Switzerland, Uruguay and the United States (partial).

REFERENCES

Asthana, A. (2017, April 2). Theresa May Would Go to War to Protect Gibraltar, Howard Says. *The Guardian.*

Barnier, M. (2017, November 29). *Speech by Michel Barnier at the Berlin Security Conference.* SPEECH/17/5021, Berlin.

Black, J. (2017, April 5). This Latest Gibraltar Dispute Is a Sign of Things to Come. *Prospect.* Retrieved from https://www.prospectmagazine.co.uk/world/this-latest-gibraltar-dispute-is-a-sign-of-things-to-come.

Black, J., Hall, A., Cox, K., Kepe, M., & Silversten, E. (2017). *Defence and Security After Brexit: Understanding the Possible Implications of the UK's Decision to Leave the EU.* Compendium Report, RAND Europe.

Bundesnachrichtendienst. (2018). *BND, DGSE and MI6 Emphasise Necessity of International Cooperation.* Retrieved from http://www.bnd.bund.de/EN/_Home/Startseite/Buehne_Box/Textbausteine/News_ENG/180216_MSC18/180216_MSC18_Artikel.html;jsessionid=09F8AA7423E566CB6008DD5085713E84.1_cid386?nn=3132246.

Cobain, I., & Ball, J. (2013, May 22). UK Provided More Support for CIA Rendition Flights Than Thought. *The Guardian.*

Council of the EU. (2017, May 18). *Council Conclusions on Security and Defence in the Context of the EU Global Strategy.* 9178/17, Brussels.

Court of Justice of the EU. (2015, October 6). *Judgement in Case C-362/14, Maximillian Schrems v Data Protection Commissioner.* Press Release No. 117/15, Luxembourg.

Court of Justice of the EU. (2016, September 8). *Advocate-General's Opinion in the Request for an Opinion 1/15, Court of Justice of the EU.* Press Release No. 89/16, Luxembourg.

Dassù, M., Ischinger, W., Vimont, P., & Cooper, R. (2018, March 20). *Keeping Europe Safe After Brexit.* Policy Brief, European Council on Foreign Relations, ECFR/248.

Dawson, J. (2017). *Brexit: Implications for National Security.* House of Commons Library No. CBP7798, 31 March.

Dearlove, R. (2016, March 24). EU Exit Could Make Britain Safer. *Reuters.* Retrieved from http://uk.reuters.com/article/uk-britain-eu-security/eu-exit-could-make-britain-safer-former-mi6-spy-chief-idUKKCN0WQ0NE.

Duke, S. (2014). Intelligence and EU External Relations: Operational to Constitutive Politics. In T. Blom & S. Vanhoonacker (Eds.), *The Politics of Information: The Case of the European Union.* Houndmills: Palgrave Macmillan.

Eden, G. (2015, May 6). Tempora. *Surveillance Society.* Retrieved from http://www.dcssproject.net/tempora/.

European Commission. (2017a, January 10). *Communication from the Commission to the European Parliament and the Council, Exchanging and Protecting Personal Data in a Globalised World.* COM (2017) 7 Final, Brussels.

European Commission. (2017b, December 8). *Communication from the Commission to the European Council on the State of Negotiations with the United Kingdom Under Article 50 of the Treaty on European Union.* COM (2017) 784 Final.

European Commission. (2018a, February 28). *European Commission Draft Withdrawal Agreement on the Withdrawal of the United Kingdom of Great Britain and Northern Ireland from the European Union and the European Atomic Energy Community.* TF50 (2018) 33.

European Commission. (2018b, January 24). *Internal EU27 Preparatory Discussions on the Framework for the Future Relationship: "Security, Defence and Foreign Policy".* TF50 (2018) 25.

European Parliament. (2001, July 11). *Report on the Existence of a Global System for the Interception of Private and Commercial Communications.* Part 1, A5-0264/2001.

European Parliament. (2017). *The Impact and Consequences of Brexit for Northern Ireland.* Parliamentary Briefing, Constitutional Affairs, PE 583 116. Retrieved from http://www.europarl.europa.eu/RegData/etudes/ BRIE/2017/583116/IPOL_BRI(2017)583116_EN.pdf.

House of Commons. (2016). Border Force Budget 2016–2017. *Hansard, 608,* Column 923.

House of Commons. (2017, February 22). *Third-Second Report of Session 2016–17.* Documents Considered by the European Scrutiny Committee.

House of Lords. (2015, December 9). *Hansard.* Column 1637.

House of Lords. (2016a, October 13). *Leaving the European Union: Foreign and Security Policy Cooperation.* Library Note.

House of Lords. (2016b, December 16). *Brexit: Future UK-EU Security and Police Cooperation.* European Union Committee, 7th Report of Session 2016–2017, HL Paper 77.

Migration Watch UK. (2016). *The Implications of Brexit for Border Controls in Calais.* Retrieved from https://www.migrationwatchuk.org/briefing-paper/376.

Paravicini, G. (2017, November 10). Julian King's Poison Portfolio. *Politico.* Retrieved from https://www.politico.eu/article/julian-king-brexit-eu-commissioner-uk-terrorism/.

Sawers, J. (2016). I Am a Former MI6 Chief and a Lifelong Patriot. Here's Why I'm Voting Remain. *Daily Telegraph.* Retrieved from http://www.telegraph. co.uk/news/2016/06/16/why-this-lifelong-patriot-is-voting-remain/.

UK Government. (2017a, September 18). *Security, Law Enforcement and Criminal Justice: A Future Partnership Paper.* Retrieved from https://www.

gov.uk/government/publications/security-law-enforcement-and-criminal-justice-a-future-partnership-paper.

UK Government. (2017b). *The UK's Exit from the European Union: Northern Ireland and Ireland: Position Paper*. Position Paper, Additional Data Paper CTA Travel Area Data and Statistics.

UK Government. (2017c, September). *Foreign Policy, Defence and Development: A Future Partnership Paper*.

UK Government. (2017d, January 17). *Prime Minister May's Speech: The Government's Negotiating Objectives for Exiting the EU*. Retrieved from https://www.gov.uk/government/speeches/the-governments-negotiating-objectives-for-exiting-the-eu-pm-speech.

UK Government. (2018a, February 17). *Prime Minister May's Speech at the 2018 Munich Security Conference*. Retrieved from https://www.gov.uk/government/speeches/pm-speech-at-munich-security-conference-17-february-2018.

UK Government. (2018b, July). *The Future Relationship Between the United Kingdom and the European Union*. Cm 9593.

Warrell, H. (2017, November 14). UK Opts in to New Europol Intelligence-Sharing Programme. *Financial Times*.

CHAPTER 5

Moving Beyond Brexit: Scenarios for the Future

Much of the literature on Brexit, security and defence has tended reflect British preoccupations with far less attention being accorded to the perspectives of the EU and its members which in many ways is more important since the UK is, after all, the *demandeur* (see Whitman 2017, 47–54). The value attached to any future partnership with the UK by the Union and its members is likely to hinge on the extent to which it is perceived to contribute to the EU's ability to attain a number of broad security and defence objectives. At their broadest, these aims and objectives can be found in the European Commission's March 2017 'Reflection Paper' where three scenarios for EU-27 security and defence by 2025 are presented (European Commission 2017). The first is based on loose security and defence cooperation, with the ability to carry out only modest missions and the EU complementing the efforts of the Member States. Under this scenario defence cooperation would remain a political goal, but with fragmented European defence industries and defence capabilities would continue to be generated at the national level. The second scenario, that of shared security and defence, foresees greater financial and operational solidarity with more ability to project military force externally and enabling the EU to conduct more ambitious operations. The EU would enable cooperation between the Member States which would include the sharing and merger of threat analysis and assessments. A number of capabilities would also be truly multinational, ranging from strategic transport, remotely

S. Duke, *Will Brexit Damage our Security and Defence?*,
https://doi.org/10.1007/978-3-319-96107-1_5

piloted aircraft systems, maritime surveillance and satellite communications. Finally, a common defence scenario implies that solidarity and mutual assistance between the Member States is the norm. The EU would be able to conduct high-end operations, with contingency planning carried out at the European level and greater integration of national defence forces at the European level. Forces would be pre-positioned and permanently available for rapid deployment by the EU.

Before analysing the Commission's three scenarios, two other possible outcomes deserve inclusion. First, the EU is of course not the only security actor active at the European level and the potential impact of Brexit on EU-NATO relations is also important. This could represent a fourth option for the UK, which is to privilege and deepen ties with NATO and to work within the Alliance to strengthen its European pillar with the UK as a catalyst. Finally, there is also need to consider the role and place of the numerous bilateral ties that the UK has with a number of EU members, most notably France. These are an important part of the equation and represent a fifth option, especially in the event of no deal with the EU on the terms and conditions of the UK's departure from the EU.

The five scenarios, each of which would imply a different level of engagement by the UK with the EU, as well as legal arrangements, are considered in turn.

EU Security and Defence Cooperation (with Loose UK Association)

The first scenario posits voluntary cooperation with *ad hoc* and case-by-case agreements with the EU if and when a crisis emerges (Table 5.1). This would obviously be the easiest scenario for the UK since it would open up the possibility of association, without the potential exclusivity, commitments and intrusiveness that deeper forms of EU security and defence cooperation might entail. It is assumed that this scenario is most likely in the event of a 'no deal' which, in practical terms, means the failure to successfully negotiate a comprehensive association agreement with the EU.

Association by third parties with EU missions and operations is accomplished either via a general Strategic Partnership Agreement (SPA) (Canada), a Norway-type Framework Participation Agreement (FPA) or a Swiss-style participation agreement (PA) for a specific mission or operation.[1] In each

[1] The SPA with Canada was signed 2016 but has yet to be ratified by all EU members. A similar agreement has been reached with Japan and one is under negotiation with Azerbaijan.

Table 5.1   The UK's post-transition security and defence options

UK level of engagement with EU	Type of EU instrument	Conditions of instruments	Pros for UK	Cons for UK
High	Bespoke Treaty	Legally binding & ratification by European Parl. & EU members	Reflects joint UK-EU interests & allow for some secondment and staff/exchange of classified material	Unlikely to allow UK nearer EU decision-making tables & others likely to demand similar rights if granted
High	Association Agreement	Legally binding & ratification by European Parl. & EU members	Highest level of formal dialogue and greatest chance to influence EU	UK must respect internal market, customs union and four freedoms
Medium	Strategic Partnership Agreement	Legally binding, ratification by European Parl. and EU members	High levels of dialogue that extend into home security cooperation	Normally accompanied by extensive trade agreement & not unique
Medium	Partnership & Cooperation Agreement	Legally binding and consent of Council and European Parl. needed	Less formal than Assoc. Agt. but still extensive dialogue	Designed primarily for EU's neighbouring countries & not unique
Low	Framework Participation Agreement	Legal framework for third party contributions to CSDP operations/ missions	Can be done on an case-by-case basis & demonstration of solidarity with EU	Inability to shape decisions on CSDP operation/ mission mandates & not unique
Low	Declarations/ad hoc alignment	Associate with declaration on bilateral basis	Allows for divergence when in UK interests	UK can only associate but not shape decisions & not unique

case, non-EU partners such as Canada, Iceland, Norway, Russia, Ukraine and Turkey are invited to participate by the EU in CSDP missions or operations, as well as broader alignment with CFSP positions and sanctions. Participation or alignment are then matters for national decision. Of the three, SPA's involve the most comprehensive dialogue and exchange and involve not only cooperation on international peace and security but also Justice, Freedom and Security issues. FPAs are negotiated with each third state on a case-by-case basis, which is time consuming and often difficult to finalise, especially if the operation is of short duration. This process has been sped up with the adoption of more or less standard elements to the agreements. The Swiss variant is, for all ostensible purposes, a FPA.

All agreements conform to the notion that third state contributions are 'without prejudice to the decision-making autonomy of the Union'— hence the importance of removing all UK operational command positions by the end of March 2019 (Tardy 2014, 2). Normally, involvement of third parties in CSDP operations and missions is only approved by the PSC at a relatively late stage and this does not involve participation in the drafting of the Concept of Operations (CONOPS) or the Operation Plan (OPLAN). Once invited, they are 'required to accept the EU's timeline and procedures' (Tardy 2014, 4). They are, however, normally included in a 'force generation' conference (where the decisions on the required assets and personnel are made) as well as the Committee of Contributors (CoC) which is responsible for the day-to-day conduct of the mission or operation. FPA's allow for prior agreement on liability issues arising from the conduct of EU crisis management operations, contributions to the operational budget, medical certification, the supervisory authority of the EU Commander or Head of Mission, overall authority, rights, discipline and obligations (see as an example Department of State 2011). Status of Forces (SOFA—for operations involving military) and the Status of Mission (SOMA—for civilian missions) Agreements cover the status of personnel seconded to the crisis management mission for questions of legal liability and it is also understood that non-EU members contributing to a mission or operation undertake to pay the costs associated with their participation.

Any future UK cooperation in civilian and military crisis management operations would have to be regulated through a security-oriented framework agreement—the negotiation of which may make it 'enhanced'. Norway signed a framework agreement in 2004 and has since then participated in 11 CSDP missions, versus the UK's 15 (at different levels). In addition, any exchange of classified information would also be subject to Security of Information Agreement with the EU that often accompany FPAs. It is worth briefly noting that in the NATO context five enhanced FPAs exist, but not all members are 'enthusiastic about encouraging greater involvement of partner countries for fear that it will undermine collective defence pursuant to Article 5 of the North Atlantic Treaty' (Wieslander 2014). Similar arguments could be employed on the EU side with regard to the mutual assistance clause (Article 42.7 of the Treaty on European Union).

More generally, beyond Norway, the EU has signed framework agreements with Canada, Iceland, Montenegro, Russia, Serbia, Turkey, Ukraine and US. In total, around 25 countries have contributed to 16 CSDP missions and operations (EEAS 2016). In cases like Canada, participation in CSDP missions or operations is complemented by a SPA to enable more extensive dialogue, exchange information and explore cooperation. It is worth noting that participation of non-EU countries in CSDP missions and operations is often accompanied by broader foreign policy alignment, including on sanctions.

The obvious negative of such as loose association with the EU is that it is unlikely to satisfy the UK's desire to retain access to key EU agencies that are of importance to the UK's national security, like Europol, since this would only be possible in the context of a deeper and more comprehensive association agreement. Whether it is possible to negotiate a looser *agreement*, covering the external dimensions of EU-UK defence and security, and a specific *treaty* for the internal security aspects, without it appearing that London is engaged in cherry-picking, remains to be seen.

Shared EU Security and Defence (with Closer UK Involvement)

There have been demands for close post-Brexit UK involvement in EU security and defence, normally justified on the grounds of 'the UK's larger role in foreign affairs and its defence contribution' (Blunt 2017, 6–7). This would normally involve negotiating some form of legally-binding Partnership and Cooperation Agreement (PCA) with the EU which would lay down the general principles, broad agreement on dialogue, the promotion of shared objectives and to lay the basis for various forms of cooperation in sectoral policy areas (including the economic, security and cross-cutting dimensions of the partnership) (Table 5.1). This would be a bilateral treaty, but could also include commitments to coordinate in various multilateral fora, like NATO or the UN. It could also, conceivably, take the form of a Canada or Japan-type SPA, but it should be noted that in both cases these have been negotiated alongside a comprehensive trade agreement; the obvious implication being that the failure of any party to satisfactorily negotiate and ratify an economic and trade agreement could have negative implications for a prospective SPA.

A PCA-type agreement would move the UK and the EU closer than the first scenario in those areas of mutual interest, but it would be less ambitious than a full association agreement (normally used for EU candidates or those with a customs union with the EU). A PCA would, however, be unsuitable for some forms of cooperation that have been proposed such as the UK being granted observer status to the PSC, as was demanded by Crispin Blunt MP. Even if the UK were to embark upon unparalleled cooperation with the EU, it is hard to conceive of the ambassadors of the EU27 being comfortable with the idea of an observer especially since, as Blunt envisages, any such status should extend to speaking rights in discussions and the right to place items on the agenda. The European Commission has ruled out any such arrangement during any agreed transition period and beyond.

With regard to the Foreign Affairs Council, where the UK will not be represented post-Brexit, Blunt suggests six monthly informal meetings of the Foreign Ministers with the British Foreign Secretary organised under the auspices of the rotating Council Presidency, supplemented by regular meetings with the High Representative on a monthly or quarterly basis. Once again, this may not be the exclusive partnership that the UK seeks since the European Economic Area (EEA) agreement already facilitates biannual political dialogue on foreign policy, meetings with the foreign ministers and the EU Presidency foreign minister twice a year, as well as meetings between the heads of government. *Ad hoc* meetings are also scheduled with the High Representative/Vice-President. In addition, the EEA countries are invited to align themselves with CFSP common positions, declarations and often sanctions. In a similar manner, Norway has seconded national experts to the EEAS for election observation and support, democracy and human rights.[2] Whether these are the areas that the UK may wish to second national experts is open to doubt. It therefore remains uncertain whether the EU will grant the UK the kind of exclusive arrangement it wishes for, especially in the face of the experience of the EEA members and their coordination with the EU.

A PCA would have the benefit of flexibility and less commitment than an association agreement but it could exclude the UK from association or

[2] The non-EU European Economic Area countries (Iceland, Liechtenstein and Norway) are all entitled to become Seconded National Experts in the EU's institutions.

membership of EU agencies, like the EDA. This would imply that post-Brexit the UK would have to surrender its place on the EDA's Steering Board, but it would also imply that it would not be obliged to pay the £3–4 million in contributions per year (this would create a considerable dent in the EDA's budget since contributions are calculated on a sliding GNI scale). Continued participation in Europol activities, and access to the relevant databases, could also be problematic and British universities and research establishments may also lose access to European Research Council funding.

A Common EU Defence and Security (with Quasi-Membership Involvement for the UK)

Under this scenario the EU would deepen integration towards a genuine common defence and security on the basis of a bespoke agreement (Table 5.1). This is the kind of integration that President Emmanuel Macron, as well as the EPP in the European Parliament and Germany and Italy have called for. The political underpinnings of the advocacy for a European Defence Union, a Schengen for Defence, or whatever it may eventually be called, all point in this direction.

This scenario would most likely be part of a negotiated association agreement with the EU which would typically involve more extensive and deeper commitments than the PCA referred to above. This is also what the UK has asked for (UK Government 2018a, 84–5). The UK government's suggestion is that this could consist of a number of agreements, with some legally binding (like a core Free Trade Agreement and aspects of internal security), while others could be based upon looser 'political commitments', such as components of external security cooperation, complemented by a suitable institutional structure. The 25 existing association agreements are primarily aimed at convergence of a third party (like Georgia, Moldova or Ukraine) with the EU's internal market and thus tend to concentrate heavily on trade, investment and regulatory convergence. They go beyond the simple cooperation found in PCAs to include closer economic and political convergence, based upon most favoured nation treatment and a privileged partnership. Typically, security and defence are not addressed in any depth in the existing agreements except in so far as it promotes the general 'convergence' of the third party with the EU (the security aspects may, however, be subject to a separate

FPA as in the cases of Canada and Norway). Ironically, a number of countries with association agreements have complained that they offer all of the burdens of conforming to the *acquis* with none of the benefits of membership. Such agreements are generally designed to 'encourage convergence on the EU acquis and to enhance political co-operation', whereas the purpose of any British deal will be to manage 'divergence from the acquis and to downgrade political co-operation' (House of Commons 2018, 23). The European Parliament's Brexit Steering Group preference, as outlined in March 2018, is for an association agreement with the UK covering trade, internal security, cooperation on foreign policy and defence and other thematic cooperation. This scenario would, however, oblige the UK to respect the integrity of the internal market, customs union and the four freedoms, without allowing for cherry-picking. It would also preserve the EU's decision-making and legal order, including the role of the ECJ. The UK government's July 2018 White Paper makes it quite clear on several occasions that it intends to end the free movement of people, thus violating one of the European Parliament's red lines (UK Government 2018a, 32). It also makes it clear that it will end the jurisdiction of the ECJ, except when it applies to an agency that the UK participates in.

It remains to be seen if the UK can feasibly leverage its military, intelligence and security capabilities and expertise as part of a tailored association agreement with the EU to help reach mutually agreed goals. The febrile internal politics within the UK and its political parties, when combined with red lines drawn by Brussels, makes the prospects for an association agreement of the type outlined by the UK government distant. Any such agreement would also be likely to carry EU demands for up-front assurances to the EU27 that the UK would not disrupt closer European integration in security and defence. This may prove to be a hard sell, given the UK's mixed record in CSDP. But, with such an assurance the UK may be able to negotiate some form of enhanced partnership on security and defence as part of a wider association agreement but, in the context of more tightly integrated EU security and defence, it would also give the UK less room for manoeuvre. It may also prove to be politically compromising for any UK government who, at least implicitly, appeared to support the formation of some form of European Defence Union.

On the UK's future post-Brexit cooperation on CSDP specifically, the Norwegian model is again instructive. Norway signed an administrative agreement with the EDA in 2006, but it can only participate in projects by invite, nor do they play a role in the discussions where new projects are conceived and shaped. Similar agreements have been concluded by the EDA with Switzerland (2012), Serbia (2013) and Ukraine (2015). Any special status for the post-Brexit UK in the EDA, or any other EU agency would, it is assumed, be accompanied by an appropriate financial contribution and it may also be contingent upon the UK accepting freedom of movement. Moreover, any such agreement would inevitably lead to demands for similar treatment by the countries mentioned above.

Any progression towards this most ambitious form of security and defence integration will depend heavily on France which will have to be the mainstay for the formation of any common intervention force, provide the lion's share of any common budget as well as inspiration at the strategic and doctrinal levels. This implies that the UK's bilateral relations with France will be particularly important in determining the degree of UK participation in any common EU security and defence, just as it was in determining the UK's membership of the European Communities in the first place.

THE UK REBUILDS AND STRENGTHENS THE 'EUROPEAN PILLAR' IN NATO

This scenario is not necessarily excluded by any of the preceding ones since the UK could choose to do this in addition to redefining its relations with the EU. Historically, the UK has taken a strong Atlanticist position, stressing that any security and defence integration at the European pillar should serve to strengthen NATO and its transatlantic ties. This was the spirit in which the UK helped lay the political foundations for what became CSDP in St Malo in 1998. Even if there was ambiguity about the nature of any 'autonomous' EU military capabilities agreed to in the joint declaration between President Chirac and Prime Minister Blair, the UK was nevertheless confident that the St Malo initiative would strengthen the EU and its credibility vis-à-vis NATO and the United States. At the time this was seen as a positive measure to develop the European Security and Defence Initiative (ESDI) or the European Pillar within the Atlantic Alliance.

Having played such an important initial role, the UK became far less enthusiastic about CSDP in the more recent years. Three main reasons can be suggested. First, once created the UK had limited ability to influence the growth and direction of CSDP. A critical turning point was the question of what would happen to the Western European Union (WEU) which, in the Maastricht Treaty, had been responsible for the elaboration and implementation of decisions and actions that have defence implications. The gradual assumption by the EU of many of the functions of the WEU, including its role in defence, saw the formal end of the WEU in the 2000 Marseilles Declaration (Western European Union 2000). Of less public note was the simultaneous vanishing of ESDI where the WEU had formed a visible 'European pillar'.

Second, the assumption that the relatively new CSDP and NATO would develop in a complementary manner was further challenged by the accession of the Republic of Cyprus to the EU in 2004. This effectively cast into doubt existing sharing arrangements agreed to between the EU and NATO under the 2002 "Berlin Plus" arrangements since any such loaning of assets from NATO to the EU, or the exchange of classified information, would involve the assent of all NATO members (including Turkey). The fact that all EU members are either NATO members or members of its Partnership for Peace, with the notable exception of Cyprus, has been a severe impediment to the development of EU-NATO relations.

Third, U.S. support for CSDP has been historically ambivalent. Various versions of Secretary of State Madeleine Albright's exhortations, shortly after the St Malo Declaration, that any European initiatives in security and defence should avoid de-linking (of ESDI from NATO), duplication (of existing efforts in NATO) and discrimination (against non-EU members)—known as the three 'D's'—neatly summarise the Alliance's concerns with the development of CSDP (Albright 1998). Conservative thinkers in the U.S. continue to caution against possible rifts in transatlantic solidarity that may be caused by CSDP with a recent call for 'NATO-centric solutions ensuring that all advancements in European defense capabilities are done through NATO or at least on a multilateral basis' (Coffey 2017). The UK has been particularly sensitive to initiatives by the EU or its members that could violate one of Albright's '3 D's', such as the 2003 Belgium, France and Germany proposals to create a dedicated EU military headquarters. These sensitivities have not completely waned although the UK's voice has already been diluted on CSDP issues. For instance, under normal circumstances, the MPCC would have fallen under the 'duplication' category for the UK and would have been blocked as it was in 2003, but instead the proposal was watered down (to an advisory role for non-executive missions) and was subject to politically driven delays over language by the UK, especially the use of the term 'operational headquarter' (Barigazzi 2017).

It should be noted that the UK is not alone in its reservations about specific aspects of CSDP, or its direction of growth vis-à-vis NATO. Brexit will, however, imply that those with reservations, like Denmark, Ireland and some of the Baltic and Scandinavian countries, may now have to make their concerns known. The UK will be able to continue to work with like-minded countries, such as Portugal, the Netherlands and Spain, to ensure close connections between the EU and NATO.

The possibility of serious EU-NATO institutional rifts has been attenuated somewhat by the common set of proposals for the implementation of the 2016 Joint EU-NATO Declaration which now cover 74 items spread over seven issue areas ranging from hybrid threats, to cyber defence, defence industry and research to exercises (NATO 2016). But, in spite of portraying the EU and NATO as 'natural partners', NATO's Secretary-General, Jens Stoltenberg, echoed former US Secretary of State Madeleine Albright's twenty-year-old warning that EU's defence efforts carry 'The risk of weakening the transatlantic bond, the risk of duplicating what NATO is already doing and the risk of discriminating against non-EU members of the NATO Alliance' (Stoltenberg 2018).

As a soon to be non-member of the EU, the UK will play an important role in shaping EU-NATO relations either by either reinforcing the Albright-Stoltenberg cautionary approach to EU security and defence efforts, or if Prime Minister May's desire for a relationship of unprecedented 'depth and breadth' is to be taken at face value, by drawing the EU and NATO closer together. The UK government has indicated that 'NATO will remain the cornerstone of European defence and security' and that it is willing to cooperate on security and defence with the EU, but in ways that enhance coherence with the Alliance (UK Government 2018a, 81). Whichever way is chosen, it should be borne in mind that the UK's influence in both the EU and NATO on security and defence matters is likely to decline as a result of Brexit. For instance, under the EU-NATO 'Berlin Plus' agreement it was agreed that, in the event of the agreement being activated, the EU may request that NATO make available a European command option for an EU-led military operation. The Deputy Supreme Allied Commander European (DSACEUR) has been the obvious candidate for such a command. By tradition, going back to 1951 and thus pre-dating the European Communities, the DSACEUR has been British. This arrangement serves as an explicit link between NATO and the EU in *Operation Althea* which began in 2004 in Bosnia and Herzegovina and which falls under the current DSACEUR.

His responsibilities for operational command will have to be transferred by the end of March 2019 since a UK incumbent will be unable to offer NATO assets to EU missions under the Berlin Plus agreement. In recognition of the loss of the DSACEUR position the UK lobbied heavily, and successfully, for the appointment of Air Chief Marshal Stuart Peach, chief of the UK's armed forces, as the chair of NATO's Military Committee.

At a less symbolic level, the UK's potential loss of influence over defence-related research and development, which it enjoyed through its membership of EDA, will depend upon its ability to negotiate a bespoke agreement. Any such agreement though is unlikely to allow the UK to play a privileged role over and above that of the current associates. The likely loss of the ability to shape and, to a certain extent steer the EU's research agenda, comes at a critical juncture for the EU and NATO. Uncertainties over the UK's defence budget and its possible loss of wider international standing may further erode the UK's standing in the Alliance (see Hastings Dunn and Webber 2017).

Finally, those of a critical disposition may observe that this does little to resolve the political divisions between the EU and NATO caused by the Cyprus problem. In spite of the UK's leverage with Cyprus and Turkey, there is little to suggest that the UK has been instrumental in resolving the dispute as an EU or NATO member (see Chap. 4).

The UK Stresses Bilateral Security and Defence Ties

The UK government's ability to project and defence its interests will apparently depend upon 'a breadth of partnership that extends far beyond the institutional mechanisms for cooperation with the EU' (UK Government 2018b). One key feature in this regard are the bilateral relations with France, agreed to in the 2010 Lancaster House Treaties on defence cooperation are of particular importance. The treaties propose wider-ranging cooperation on military doctrine, personnel exchange, common procurement programmes, training, capability pooling, as well as defence industrial cooperation designed to mutually enhance technology and to lower costs. But, for the most part the treaties are non-binding (with the exception of those parts referring to the safety of nuclear warheads). Other proposals since then have been forwarded to further enhance bilateral cooperation, such as the proposal for the integration of their respective missile industries around MBDA.[3] To date, joint projects have led to less auspicious results such as the French plan to purchase the British-made Watchkeeper drones, used in the British armed forces, which was abandoned in preference for Patroller drones made by a French company, Safran Electronics and Defence. For its part, the British Army declined to purchase the *Véhicule Blindé de Combat d'Infanterie* when France chose not to purchase Watchkeeper.

Nevertheless, the Anglo-French treaties have yielded results, most notably with the creation of the 10,000 strong Combined Joint Expeditionary Force. The force has air, land and maritime components and is intended to contribute to EU, NATO or UN missions. Several exercises, including the full validation 2016 *Griffin Strike* exercise, have taken place involving the different components of the force which have 'demonstrated officially the high degree of interoperability between the two armies' (Ghez et al. 2017, 5). Joint operations in Libya in 2011, as well as British logistical support for operations in the Central African Republic and Mali and the commitment of French troops to the UK-led NATO battlegroup in Estonia in 2019, have underscored this point. Yet, it is worth noting that the combined reluctance of France and the UK to commit ground forces did little to restore security to post-Gaddafi Libya and may well have fuelled conflict across the Sahel as arms fell into the hands of *jihadi* groups.

The public stance taken by the French Minister of Defence, Jean-Yves Le Drian, that the Brexit vote will not affect military cooperation with the UK, is acknowledgement of the UK's importance to European security, including from outside the EU (Agence France Presse 2016). More pragmatically however, the emergence of a post-Brexit EU with France as the main security and defence actor and the only EU member with nuclear weapons and a permanent seat on the UN, implies that France will have to fine-tune its bilateral and European priorities. It may also suggest that France will wish to recalibrate its relationship with the U.S. to reflect this status, especially since during the Obama administration France 'emerged as America's most willing and capable military partner, partly because of UK politics and the British preoccupation with Brexit. France effectively replaced the UK as our go-to partner when it came to missions in Africa and also kinetic operations in the Middle East, particularly Syria' (Taylor

---

[3] MDBA is a multi-national group with the chief shareholders being Airbus, BAE Systems and Leonardo.

2017, 29). It remains to be seen how the UK will adjust to this new reality, although as P5 members France and the UK will have an incentive to consult and coordinate wherever possible on multilateral issues.

If problems between France and the UK can be foreseen, they are more likely to rest at the strategic and multilateral levels. At the strategic level France has been particularly active in promoting CSDP missions and operations in the Sahel and Sub-Saharan Africa. In the ten cases where the UK has *not* contributed to CSDP missions or operations, all but one (a monitoring mission in Georgia) have been in either the Sahel or sub-Saharan Africa (four have been in the Central African Republic and four in the Democratic Republic of the Congo). The UK's interests have tended to be far more oriented to maritime missions and, geographically, towards the Western Balkans, Iraq and Afghanistan. The UK's pattern of involvement is not confined to the EU since contributions to UN peace keeping operations show similar patterns; the UK does not see itself as an ordinary contributor to UN operations and prefers to use its military or high-end operations like Sierra Leone or Iraq, rather than contributing rank and file infantry. In both the EU and UN cases it is apparent that the UK does not share their assessments of the significance of sub-Saharan Africa.

In a speech at the Sorbonne in September 2017 President Macron advocated that, 'At the beginning of the next decade, Europe needs to establish a common intervention force, a common defence budget, with a common doctrine for action' (Sandford 2017). Macron's speech and the French Strategic Review of Defence and National Security the following month both promoted the European Intervention Initiative (EII) as a project to be launched 'with partners that have the necessary military capabilities and political will', on the basis of a shared European strategic culture (Revue Stratégique 2017, 63). The EII could also be read as a French hedge against the current EU defence plans, especially PESCO, which will take a long time to come to fruition. Unlike PESCO, EII is more exclusive by design and is targeted at operational effectiveness rather than PESCO's inclusive smaller-scale capability development. Although this may open up important possibilities for cooperation between France and the UK outside the EU, it also puts Whitehall in the familiar bind it has experienced with France's historic advocacy of strategic autonomy. The UK traditionally supported the development of 'a coherent full spectrum force package' in the EU context in order to bolster the EU's attractiveness to Atlantic allies, whilst also reinforcing NATO's enduring role as the 'cornerstone of collective defence for its members' (Council of the EU 2017, Annex 1).

France is likely to welcome some form of middle-way where the UK can 'opt in' to defence and security arrangements and the EII opens the possibility for multilateral cooperation outside the EU and NATO which may attract others, like Norway or Spain. The EII is likely to build upon the framework nation concept where a larger and more capable country, such as France, Germany or the UK can provide the backbone of the operational capabilities, to which other politically willing but less able allies can contribute. In this regard the UK, even with its diminishing but still substantial military resources, is of obvious attraction to France. Any such UK-French EII cooperation could build on the pragmatic spirit of the 2010 agreement which has its foundations no so much in a budding spirit of cooperation but on the 'basis of the governments' acknowledgement of economic hardship rather than long-time friendship or a wish to start a new Europe-wide defence cooperation' (Pannier 2013, 546). As valuable as the UK's association with the EII would be for Paris, German cooperation is still critical to make the link between the EII and the EU.

The French challenge will be to keep the UK connected to European security and defence, especially if the UK drops out of the EU with no deal in place, and to keep it in balance with the joint defence industrial ambitions that France and Germany hold to build an advance European fighter jet and other systems. France could decide to become the core of a network of bilateral defence partnerships, where the agreement with the UK would be but one. This network could be utilised either in the EU or NATO contexts but, in either context, with France as the key pivot. The UK will have to step-up the frequency and intensity of its bilateral relations with France in order to mitigate against strategic drift.

The UK's bilateral security and defence relations with Germany are also important due, in no small part, to the presence of nearly 10,000 British military personnel in Germany. But, they will be gradually downsized by 2020, leaving a residual presence that could serve as the basis for multilateral and bilateral exercises in the Baltics or Poland. The UK maintains an active dialogue with Germany on equipment and capabilities at the ministerial level, with the idea of increasing defence industrial collaboration and to reduce overall costs. Germany's 2016 White Paper on Security Policy refers glowingly to the 'security partnership with the United Kingdom' and the 'aim to further expand in all areas of common interest' (Germany Federal Government 2016, 80). Britain's role in creating the Joint Expeditionary Force with Denmark, Estonia, Finland, Latvia, Lithuania, the Netherlands, Norway and Sweden is also mentioned positively in the policy paper as an example of the UK's ability to form the backbone for a variety of flexible coalitions (six of whom are EU members and the same number are NATO members). Against this, however, it is worth noting how seldom the UK is otherwise mentioned in the White Paper as well as the enthusiasm with which the German Defence and Foreign Ministers took up the political call for a European Security and Defence Union with their French counterparts. There are also signs that the UK wishes to cooperate more closely with Spain post-Brexit on a variety of military and non-military security issues but progress in this regard is likely to be influenced by the ability of both parties to reach an understanding on access at the Gibraltar-Spain border.

The UK's growing reliance upon bilateral security ties post Brexit was symbolised by the signature of a Treaty on Defence and Security Cooperation with Poland in December 2017. This not only builds upon the deployment of UK troops to Poland as part of NATO's Enhanced Forward Presence but goes beyond this to include cooperation against Russian disinformation, cyber security, defence industrial and capability development, information sharing and training (UK Government 2017a). The Polish agreement, alongside the reinforced bilateral Anglo-French military and security ties following President Macron's first UK visit in January 2018 and the prospect of a forthcoming Anglo-German statement on future defence cooperation, point not only at the importance of bilateral agreements for the UK but also efforts by Prime Minister May to reassure the EU27 about Britain's unconditional commitment to European security.

Cooperation through bilateral and other *ad hoc* mechanisms cannot therefore be ruled out as a way of keeping the UK involved in CSDP and other aspects of the EU's external security, but with the wider issue of the extent to which any such cooperation can be formalised remains an open question. If history is an accurate guide, bilateral cooperation will tend to be viewed by London through the extent to which it strengthens NATO and the Alliance's right of first refusal, as per its understanding of the Anglo-French 1998 St Malo Declaration, and in second place the extent to which such cooperation supports EU crisis management.

CONCLUSIONS

The UK will remain actively involved in European security. That much is clear. It is also clear that dialogue between the EU and UK will continue. What is less obvious is how and in what capacity. Although there remain significant ambiguities and questions about the UK's future relations with the EU, as well as whether the EU is likely to attain its bold ambitions in security and defence, three conclusions in the form of propositions can be offered.

First, **the UK is important to the EU's future security and defence, but not as important as it thinks**. The legal and operational conclusions of the UK becoming a 'third country' in defence and security terms are that the defence minister will no longer take part in meetings of EU defence ministers; there will be no ambassador sitting in the PSC; the UK will not be a able to take command of EU-led operations or serve as the framework nation for Union battlegroups; it will not be a member of the EDA or Europol; it will not be able to benefit from the EDF in the same way as the Member States; nor will the UK be involved in decision-making or planning EU defence and security (Barnier 2017). The UK's bargaining power may, as Barnier noted, be limited due to the fact that the UK 'has not been the spearhead of European defence' representing barely 5% of the personnel deployed on EU-led military operations, alongside its longer-term resistance to setting up a European headquarters or turning the EU into a military power.

Any future partnership will therefore be framed by three principles: a third country may not lay claim to a status that is equivalent or superior to that of a Member of the Union; the Union's decision-making autonomy must be respected; any voluntary participation of the UK in European defence will 'confer rights and obligations in proportion to the level of this participation' (Barnier 2017; European Commission 2018b). Nevertheless, it is possible that mechanisms will be developed for 'closer and more constant coordination with non-European Union countries and international organisations' involved in EU missions and operations (Mogherini 2017). The exact nature of these 'mechanisms' is not yet clear, but they may well be shaped by the forthcoming negotiations with the UK on the internal and external aspects of security. Whatever mechanisms are negotiated, they are unlikely to be exclusive to the UK since others with shared security concerns, like Norway, may well demand similar status if preferable to their existing agreements.

Second, **the UK clearly needs the EU for aspects of its own national security**. The case for some form of unique partnership from the UK side is based on the availability of 'assets, capabilities and influence to the EU and European partners' (UK Government 2017b, 18). It is, however, clear from the earlier analysis that the UK also needs the EU in a number of ways ranging from access to databases relating to terrorism, organised crime, trafficking and cyber security. This, in essence, is what Prime Minister May has proposed in the form of a 'new Treaty to underpin our future *internal* security relationship' (UK Government 2018b, emphasis added). As it stands, the Draft Withdrawal Agreement rules out UK access to networks, information systems or data bases established under Union law from the end of the transition period (European Commission 2018a, 6). By way of distinction, the UK's desire is to address its future external security (notably CSDP) relations with the EU through a vaguer political commitment. The UK's position reflects the distinct legal status of CFSP/CSDP in the treaties which contrast with the rights and duties of the European institutions (including the Court) found in other policy areas (UK Government 2018b). The chance of some form of political commitment for CSDP is relatively high since it will be relatively straightforward to negotiate, although there may still be contentious issues like UK access to the EDA, PESCO and the EDF. This contrasts with Justice and Home Affairs (covering the internal security aspects) which is a shared EU competence and an area where the UK has signified its desire for a legally binding agreement covering the core areas of trade as well internal security. In order to reach such an agreement potentially tricky questions relating to data protection, the role of the European Court of Justice (ECJ) and the observance of key EU fundamental freedoms will have to be resolved. It remains to be seen whether the core components, such as trade and internal security, are intrinsically linked in the eyes of the negotiating partners.

The prospect of a looser political commitment addressing CSDP, will not only be easier to negotiate but may also have positive knock-on effects for the more complicated prospective agreement on internal security. Reaching the latter will be far more complicated and will not merely be a matter of avoiding 'rigid institutional restrictions or deep-seated ideology' as May stated in her speech to the Munich Security Conference (UK Government 2018b). The challenges of finding a 'principled but pragmatic solution to close legal-cooperation' which respects the UK's 'unique status as a third country with our own sovereign legal order' will also imply respect for the Union's legal order and this will demand clarity on the post-Brexit role of the ECJ (UK Government 2018b). There is, however, some room for optimism since in the same speech May stated that, 'when participating in EU agencies, the UK will respect the remit of the European Court of Justice', whereas it was something that has been categorically rejected a year earlier in the Prime Minister's Lancaster House speech where 'control of our own laws' was one of the government's guiding principles (UK Government 2017c, 2018). This is a pivotal issue for any EU-UK treaty on the internal aspects of security and will require, in the first place, an appreciation of the potential mutual security benefits stemming from post-Brexit collaboration and, by the same token, the costs of non-agreement.

Third, **the UK risks losing influence in not only the EU but NATO as well**. The assumption that the UK will be able to 're-balance' its European security role through NATO is unsound. At least in symbolic terms the UK is likely to lose influence in NATO with the potential appointment of a non-British DSACEUR and the real danger that adverse post-Brexit economic adversity will see the UK struggling to meet the 2% of GDP goal. Even if the UK continues to meet this goal, overall defence expenditure may shrink in real terms as the post-Brexit economy contracts. Historically, the security role of the UK in the EU was valued by Washington, but with the prospect of the UK leaving the EU this influence too will diminish and cannot be replicated via NATO. The UK cannot therefore count on indefinitely being 'America's closest partner' as May maintains (UK Government 2018b). If a new 'special relationship' emerges in security and defence with the U.S. it is most likely to be with France (and possibly with Germany in other policy areas, although this is open to doubt under the Trump administration).

The UK's future participation in EU defence and security is likely to lie in voluntary participation in CSDP missions and operations, quite possibly in EDA joint armaments programmes and capabilities projects, as well as in exchanges between intelligence services. The extent to which this can be negotiated as part of a broader package on the UK's relations with the EU remains to be seen. The outcome of the security dimensions will to an extent depend on progress on an agreement on post-Brexit trade relations, but it would be a serious mistake to leave the security dimensions as an add-on issue. It would also be a mistake to think that an EU-UK security treaty can be secured in isolation from other areas of negotiation, such as space or research, which have their own security implications. The dispute over the Galileo Global Satellite Navigation Sytem, where the EU informed the UK that post-Brexit some of Galileo's functions would no longer be available and the UK threatened in response to create an independent system, is not an auspicious omen for any wider security talks.

The issue of whether this will result in a unique partnership remains to be seen, as does the question of whether the UK's 'unconditional commitment' to European security will convince the EU27. The UK's position thus far has been built around the desire to retain a number of existing elements of its membership relations with the EU, while the Brussels mind-set often starts from the assumption that the UK wishes to leave the EU and it is therefore a case of the UK trying to upgrade its non-member status. All of this is set against the backdrop of a dynamic EU in security and defence terms that has moved, at least conceptually, beyond Brexit. By way of contrast, the UK has not really outlined any compelling post-Brexit strategic vision for itself beyond the vagaries of 'Global Britain', which is unlikely to be attained by becoming less European. A meeting of minds is necessary for mutual security and defence and it could do worse than start with the recognition that it is not in the interests of the EU to have an enfeebled and introverted UK on its doorstep; nor, by the same token, is it in the interests of the UK to obstruct closer security and defence cooperation at the European level.

<h1 style="text-align:center">REFERENCES</h1>

Agence France Presse. (2016, July 1). Brexit: La coopération militaire franco-britannique pas menace. *L'Orient Le Jour.* Retrieved from http://www.lorientlejour.com/article/994379/brexit-la-cooperation-militairefranco-britannique-pas-menacee-paris.html.

Albright, M. (1998, December 8). *Secretary Albright's Remarks to the North Atlantic Council.*

Barigazzi, J. (2017, May 17). Boris Johnson Plays Down Spat Over EU Military Unit. *Politico.*

Barnier, M. (2017, November 29). *Speech by Michel Barnier at the Berlin Security Conference.* SPEECH/17/5021.

Blunt, C. (2017). *Post-Brexit EU-UK Cooperation on Foreign and Security Policy.* Retrieved from https://www.blunt4reigate.com/sites/www.blunt4reigate.com/files/2017-04/Post-Brexit%20EU-UK%20cooperation%20on%20foreign%20%26%20security%20policy%20April%202017.pdf.

Coffey, L. (2017, June 6). *EU Defense Integration: Undermining NATO, Transatlantic Relations and European Security.* Report Europe, The Heritage Foundation.

Council of the EU. (2017, November 13). *Notification on Permanent Structured Cooperation to the Council and the High Representative of the Union for Foreign Affairs and Security Policy.* Annex 1, Principles of PESCO.

Department of State. (2011, May 17). *Framework Agreement Between the United States of America and the European Union on the Participation of the United*

States of America in European Union Crisis Management Operations. Washington. Retrieved from https://www.state.gov/documents/organization/169505.pdf.

EEAS. (2016, July 8). *CSDP Structure, Instruments and Agencies.*

European Commission. (2017, June 7). *Reflection Paper on the Future of European Defence.*

European Commission. (2018a, February 28). *European Commission Draft Withdrawal Agreement on the Withdrawal of the United Kingdom of Great Britain and Northern Ireland from the European Union and the European Atomic Energy Community.* TF50 (2018) 33.

European Commission. (2018b, January 24). *Internal EU27 Preparatory Discussions on the Framework for the Future Relationship: "Security, Defence and Foreign Policy".* TF50 (2018) 25.

European Parliament. (2016, February). Financing of CSDP Missions and Operations. *At a Glance.*

Germany Federal Government. (2016, June). *White Paper on Germany Security Policy and the Future of the Bundeswher.*

Ghez, J., Kirchner, M., Shurkin, M., Knack, A., Hall, A., & Black, J. (2017). *Defence and Security After Brexit: A Snapshot of International Perspectives on the Implications of the UK's Decision to Leave the EU.* RAND Europe, p. 5.

Hastings Dunn, D., & Webber, M. (2017). The UK, the European Union and NATO: Brexit's Unintended Consequences. *Global Affairs, 2*(5), 471–480.

House of Commons. (2018, April 4). *The Future of UK-EU Relationship.* Exiting the European Union Committee, Fourth Report of Session 2017–19, HC 935.

Mogherini, F. (2017, December 13). *Speech by the HR/VP Federica Mogherini at the "Building on Vision, Forward to Action: Delivering on EU Security and Defence" Event.* Brussels. Retrieved from https://eeas.europa.eu/headquarters/headquarters-homepage/37355/speech-hrvp-federica-mogherini-%E2%80%9Cbuilding-vision-forward-action-delivering-eu-security-and_en.

NATO. (2016, December 6). *Annex: Common Set of Proposals for the Implementation of the Joint Declaration by the President of the European Council, the President of the European Commission and the Secretary General of the North Atlantic Treaty Organization.* Press Release (2016) 178.

Pannier, A. (2013). Understanding the Working of Interstate Cooperation in Defence: An Exploration into Franco-British Cooperation After the Signing of the Lancaster House Treaty. *European Security, 22*(4), 540–558.

Revue Stratégique. (2017, October). *Revue Stratégique De Défense et de Sécurité Nationale.* DICoD Bureau des Éditions.

Sandford, A. (2017, September 26). Macron Outlines Sweeping EU Reform Plans. *Euronews.*

Stoltenberg, J. (2018, February 16). *Remarks by NATO Secretary General Jens Stoltenberg at the Opening Session of the Munich Security Conference.* Retrieved from https://www.nato.int.

Tardy, T. (2014, March). *CSDP: Getting Third States on Board.* Brief Issue, EU Institute for Security Studies, No. 6.

Taylor, P. (2017, April). *Crunch Time: France and the Future of European Defence.* Brussels: Friends of Europe.

UK Government. (2017a, December 21). *PM Announces Landmark New Package of Defence and Security Cooperation with Poland.* Retrieved from https://www.gov.uk/government/news/pm-announces-landmark-new-package-of-defence-and-security-cooperation-with-poland.

UK Government. (2017b). *Foreign Policy, Defence and Development: A Future Partnership Paper.*

UK Government. (2017c, January 17). *Prime Minister May's Speech: The Government's Negotiating Objectives for Exiting the EU.* Retrieved from https://www.gov.uk/government/speeches/the-governments-negotiating-objectives-for-exiting-the-eu-pm-speech.

UK Government. (2018a, July). *The Future Relationship Between the United Kingdom and the European Union.* Cm 9593.

UK Government. (2018b, February 17). *Prime Minister May's Speech at the 2018 Munich Security Conference.* Retrieved from https://www.gov.uk/government/speeches/pm-speech-at-munich-security-conference-17-february-2018.

Western European Union. (2000, November 13). *Marseille Declaration.* Marseille: WEU Council of Ministers.

Whitman, R. G. (2017). Avoiding a Hard Brexit in Foreign Policy. *Survival,* 59(6), 47–54.

Wieslander, A. (2014, December 18). NATO Turns Its Gaze to the Baltic Region. *EurActiv.*

Correction to: Will Brexit Damage our Security and Defence?

Correction to:
S. Duke, *Will Brexit Damage our Security and Defence?*
https://doi.org/10.1007/978-3-319-96107-1

The book was inadvertently published with incorrect Figure 1.1 and 2.1. The figures have been updated in the book.

The updated online version of the book can be found at
https://doi.org/10.1007/978-3-319-96107-1

E1
S. Duke, *Will Brexit Damage our Security and Defence?*,
https://doi.org/10.1007/978-3-319-96107-1_6

Glossary

CARD Coordinated Annual Review on Defence
CCTV Closed Circuit Television
COC Committee of Contributors
CONOPS Concept of Operations
CSDP Common Security and Defence Policy
CSIRT Computer Security and Incident Response Teams
CT Counter-Terrorism
CTA Common Travel Area
DPP Defence Planning Process
DSACEUR Deputy Supreme Allied Commander Europe (NATO)
EASA European Aviation Safety Agency
EAW European Arrest Warrant
EC European Communities
ECJ European Court of Justice
ECRIS European Criminal Records Information System
EDA European Defence Agency
EDAP European Defence Action Plan
EDF European Defence Fund
EEA European Economic Area
EEAS European External Action Service
EIS Europol Information System
ENISA European Union Agency for Network and Information Security

© The Author(s) 2019   95
S. Duke, *Will Brexit Damage our Security and Defence?*,
https://doi.org/10.1007/978-3-319-96107-1

EOP Enhanced Opportunity Partnership (NATO)
EPP European People's Party
ESDI European Security and Defence Initiative (NATO)
EU European Union
EUGS EU Global Strategy
EUMS European Union Military Staff
Eurodac European Dactyloscopy
Europol European Agency for Law Enforcement and Cooperation
EUSC European Union Satellite Centre
FCAS Future Combat Air System
FPA Framework Participation Agreement
GCHQ Government Communication Headquarters
HR/VP High Representative/Vice-President
IPSD Implementation Plan on Security and Defence
MoD Ministry of Defence (UK)
MPCC Military Planning and Conduct Capability
NATO North Atlantic Treaty Organisation
NIS Network and Information Security
NSA National Security Agency
OPLAN Operations Plan
PCA Partnership and Cooperation Agreement
PESCO Permanent Structured Cooperation
PNR Passenger Name Record
PSC Political and Security Committee
R&D Research and development
SBA Sovereign Base Area
SDSR Strategic Defence and Security Review (UK)
SIAC Single Intelligence and Analysis Capacity
SIS Schengen Information System
SOFA Status of Forces Agreement
SOMA Status of Mission Agreement
TEU Treaty on European Union
TFEU Treaty on the Functioning of the European Union
UN United Nations
UAV Unmanned Aerial Vehicle (or drone)
VEAT Voluntary *ex ante*
WEU Western European Union
WTO World Trade Organisation

INDEX[1]

[1] Note: Page numbers followed by 'n' refer to notes.

© The Author(s) 2019
S. Duke, *Will Brexit Damage our Security and Defence?*,
https://doi.org/10.1007/978-3-319-96107-1

Printed in the United States
By Bookmasters